MOI

Volume 4 / Issue #14

CW00924358

Artwork: Denis St. John (page 42 & 76), Matt Bradshaw (page 63)
Back Cover by Mike DeLisa, **EQUINOX** composition book, *circa* 1969.

Contributors: Eric Messina, Stephen R. Bissette, Steve Fenton, Louis Paul, Michael Hauss, John Harrison, Adam Parker-Edmondston, Dennis Capicik, Jason "Skunkape" Cook, Michael Elvidge, Troy Howarth, Christos Mouroukis, John Szpunar, Mike T. Lyddon, Christopher William Koenig, Matt Bradshaw, Steven Ronquillo, Morpho Sazbo, and Tim Paxton.

Timothy Paxton, Editor & Design Demon
Steve Fenton, Editor & Info-wrangler
Tony Strauss, Edit-fiend • Brian Harris, El Publisher de Grand Poobah

Editorializing
Resurrection of a Horror Icon...
well, sort of, um, yea, not really.

The title of this editorial is somewhat misleading, as it will be short. The often-professed "horror icon" seen above has weaseled its way into a second life. Kinda. Let me explain in a roundabout way:

The early '80s was a fun time for me, as it was a for many other horror and science fiction buffs. Not only did I have a lot of independent theaters to frequent around Ohio (we had five drive-ins and eight movie houses within fifteen to twenty minutes of driving distance from Oberlin; and even more in Columbus where I went to college), but it was also the beginning of the VHS home video boom and rental outlets were beginning to pop up everywhere, like mushrooms after a midnight rain. **SCANNERS, HORROR PLANET, THE ROAD WARRIOR, BURIAL GROUND, BLOOD BEACH, DAWN OF THE MUMMY, THE HOUSE BY THE CEMETERY, THE INCUBUS, GALAXY OF TERROR, THE HOWLING,** and **THE FUNHOUSE** were just some of the films that were released in 1981 alone, and there were loads more besides. Most of these cited titles played with older second-string films from previous seasons, making for double- to quadruple-bills. It was heaven for me and Lisa, my girlfriend at the time, who loved gory horror films. The sheer abundance of titles left little time for us to wonder about one called **THE EVIL DEAD** when we saw it was playing as the second feature to some other film whose title I honestly don't remember now. The ad-mat for **THE EVIL DEAD** was quite unassuming (well, to us at least, considering we must've seen Fulci's **ZOMBIE** a dozen times after eyeballing—so to speak—its ad in the *Cleveland Plain Dealer* movie listings): a woman struggling against a hand reaching up out of a cemetery plot to strangle her...or maybe she was being pulled into the burial ground, we didn't care. However, it was an eye-catching image for a film which we thought would be a forgettable throwaway.

Nope. It was **THE EVIL DEAD**. 'Nuff said!

The iconic image of model Bridget Hoffman, either in the publicity still seen at the top of page 2, or in the painting of said image on the theatrical poster and VHS sleeve, has remained a powerful image for horror movie fans ever since. The fiercely striking pose and somewhat surreal imagery has since lived on in other ways besides adorning walls (either framed and mounted or adhered to them with sticky tape). Sam Raimi's promo shot of a woman struggling against a clutching zombie arm has since even been incorporated/assimilated into the medium of India's incredible cut-and-paste VCD sleeve illustrations.

A bit of a primer: in India the VCD ("video compact disc") is still one of the primary ways to get movies into the hands of buyers. These cheaply mass-produced 2-disc VideoCD sets are typically packed in economical paper sleeves sealed within plastic baggies. They are only small, so their covers have to be wildly designed in order to better capture the attention of passing potential customers. More often than not, the films packaged within these crazy sleeve designs are your cheaply manufactured and, for the large part, not very well made "Grade C", adult-oriented horror or action films. Unlike their more Grade A or B cousins, these films rely on a lurid "Shock and Awe" approach to selling, rather than relying on the familiarity of a title (although, as seen on this page, many did try to pass themselves off as more famous films; for instance, director K.I. Sheikh's made-in-2000 flick **SAAMRI**, which, while mildly amusing at best, is not in any way, shape or form related to **3D SAAMRI**, the 1985 film by the Ramsays [see p.85]).

Those of you who are familiar with my writings in this magazine and *Weng's Chop* will know I love Indian cinema—even if sometimes it is more of a "love/hate" relationship! I have by now amassed quite a substantial collection of Indian VCDs and DVDs, covering all types of genres. Most of my collection consists of those weird, cheap Grade C films mentioned above. And I've bought—and still do buy—just about any title that looked like it had something to do with monsters, nagas ("cobra ladies"), and/or Hindu goddesses (I had little to go on other than the Romanized Hindi titles given for many of them, and I had to learn for myself what *bhoot, dushman, laash, pyasi, chudail, shaitaan, cheeck, raat* [etc.] actually meant). I must admit that the often times garish and vulgar VCD cover designs did their job, as I bought hundreds of titles...primarily going only by my gut feeling.

And that aforementioned iconic **EVIL DEAD** image (both the promo photo and the illustration) has been incorporated into at least a dozen designs (either on the front or the back) seen on movie packaging from India. Other Western films have been used as part of the horror film collage, too. The most popular acts of visual thievery have included Francis Ford Coppola's **BRAM**

STOKER'S DRACULA, Fulci's **ZOMBIE**, Franco's **OASIS OF THE ZOMBIES** (believe it or not!) and the same director's **FEMALE VAMPIRE**, plus assorted Don Post masks, and even fragments from covers of old issues of Forry's *Famous Monsters of Filmland*!

This is all very reminiscent of a time when I was collecting books on the occult in the 1970s, and bought a series of illustrated hardbacks called *Out of This World*. Each volume usually had one or two images copped from some horror film and altered slightly. They were just as ghoulishly great to look at as these oddball Indian movie designs are. In fact—lucky you!—I am working on a series of full-color digests which will chronicle the rise and eventual fall of these awesomely awful pieces of art.

~ **Tim Paxton**

MONSTER! MAIL

c/o Saucerman Studios, 26 West Vine St., Oberlin, OH 44074-1528 USA

Gone, But Not Forgotten: The Mayfield Theatre in Cleveland, OH. The theater opened for business in 1923, but is now closed

MONSTER! DISCOVERED...

I'm very excited to have discovered this newest volume of *Monster!* I purchased issue #11 on the strength of the cover art (incredible Gyaos vs. Gigan action) and I can honestly say that that issue far outweighed my expectations! There's nothing better for a fan of monsters, sci-fi and horror, who think they've seen everything, to find out that they haven't. *Monster!* reviews multitudes of movies that I've never heard of, or I know of but could never find (back in the '90s, I thought that I'd seen it all, then I discovered Mexican Horror-Wrestling cinema, it's kind of like that), and as a bonus you cover a pile of my favorites!

I'm also a big fan of the nostalgia factor. You and your writers seem to have experienced a lot of the same things that I have. Growing up in the '70s, we had a neighborhood theater called the Madison (between W. 93rd & W. 95th on Madison Ave. in Cleveland, OH). I was just old enough to see the tail end of double feature/children's matinees *and* the Madison's demise at the same time. I was fortunate enough to see the **GIANT SPIDER INVASION / GODZILLA VS. MEGALON** double feature (the theater gave out plastic spider rings, cheap, but the only thing that I have ever received free from a the-

ater, so cool). I also have fond memories of seeing **SINBAD AND THE EYE OF THE TIGER** and **AT THE EARTH'S CORE** at the Madison (when Peter Cushing shot an arrow into the fire-breathing monster and it exploded, the theater full of kids, including myself, let loose with an uproar I have not heard at a movie since, although I have to say that moments of **ARMY OF DARKNESS** came close; kind of a children's matinee for adults). *Cinema Treasures.org* states that the Madison closed in the mid-1980s, but I remember walking home from school in 7th grade, right before busing started, that must have been the 1978-1979 school year, and it was already closed. One day, while walking home from school, I noticed that the front door was open, so I went in. All of the seats had been torn out and the theater was packed with cars. A bit surreal, seeing all of those cars parked on the incline towards where the screen used to be. Surreal and sad... but then I thought about it and it all seemed a bit illegal, so I got the hell out of there.

After the Madison closed, we went to the mall to see movies, and it wasn't very exciting... the Mayfield Theater (on Mayfield Road near Murray Hill, Cleveland, OH) was the last bastion of cool cinema. The Mayfield showed art house and retro movies, and in the late '70s and early '80s I was able to see on the screen such marvels as **BARBERELLA, FORBIDDEN PLANET,** Tod

4

Browning's **FREAKS** and **THE FEARLESS VAMPIRE KILLERS**. I was also lucky enough to see around town, midnight showings of **NIGHT OF THE LIVING DEAD, THE BEST OF SEX AND VIOLENCE** and **THE MAZE 3D** (1953), and also regular theater showings of **JAWS** and **DAWN OF THE DEAD**. Now, you may be asking yourself how someone like me was able to see all of these movies at such tender preteen and early teen ages. The answer: I had a cool mom. Don't judge her (I know *Monster!* fans won't)!!! She let me stay up late on Friday night to watch *Hoolihan & Big Chuck* on WJW TV-8, even though I usually fell asleep. I spent most Saturday afternoons during the '70s watching *Superhost* on WUAB TV-43, and if I was being bad, my mother would threaten to send me outside!

super host

WUAB **43**
Lorain – Cleveland

Okay, I totally got off track...back to *Monster!*—I love the cover graphics, the nifty digest size, reviews of the completely obscure, and just about every other aspect. Since issue #11, I've read #7 and #5 cover to cover and am now making my way through every issue starting with #1..

Thanks *Monster!* Thanks for helping me remember when I used to have a fun time at the movies, because the movies, good or bad, were worth having a fun time at...

Yours,

Mr. Bearbomb

MONSTER! CONTRIBUTIONS:
FORMAT & GENERAL GUIDELINES

Heads up, y'all! When submitting your reviews or articles to *M!*, it would be much appreciated by we ye eds if you can please—make that *pretty please, with a cherry on top!*—follow these basic guidelines in pre-formatting your work for us (below, as a template, will be given a sample review covering most of the key elements). For starters, our standard font for all of the bulk text in the 'zine is that classy old standby, Times New Roman (a nice, easily readable serif font); for footnotes, we use the efficiently utilitarian and functional sans serif font, Calibri. As for point-sizes, no need to worry about those; we'll take care of details like that! (But we'll note them below anyway, just for the record…)

Sample review:-

THE WAR OF THE WORLDS
(= main title, bolded and all in block caps [in 18-pt. type])

Reviewed by Morpho Sazbo
(= writer's byline, bolded/italicized, with caps where applicable, as here [9-pt.])

USA, 1953. D: Byron Haskin
(= nation[s] of origin, year of production and director's credit [10-pt.])

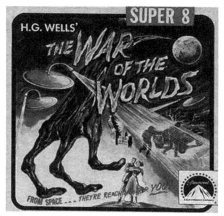

(Text should be 8-pt. and fully justified, without any tabs, with just simple line-spaces separating paragraphs. We'll set the margins. And now for our "mock-up" review…) It is tough to return to the classic, or what is often considered the classic. That said, the 1953 version of the oft-cited H.G. Wells novel *The War of the Worlds* (1898) rarely comes under any significant critical scrutiny, lest the critic be crucified for their effrontery. It is as if producer George Pal's updating of the novel's 19th Century milieu into that of the Atomic Era is a chapter etched in stone like it's the unquestionable biblical writ of "Hollywood's Take On Sci-Fi" or something. Sure, Pal's mainstream commercial filmization of **THE WAR OF THE WORLDS** does indeed have its moments, but the filmmakers' overall failure in realizing Wells' original vi-

sion is, to be frank, virtually monumental in scope. Although it doesn't come close to Orson Welles' fascinating but equally-flawed 1938 radio play, *The War of the Worlds*—which, contrary to popular misbelief, *didn't* incite nationwide panic in America, by the way; that's all since been revealed as just another urban myth—Pal's vision gets lost in his sheer love of theatrical effects, as opposed to properly dramatizing the triumph of Man over Martian as detailed in Wells' prose. If you *really* want to compare apples to oranges, then one should read not only the original source novel, but also listen to Jeff Wayne's prog-rock/orchestrated/spoken-word audio concept LP *Musical Version of The War of the Worlds* (Columbia/CBS Records, 1978), as well as watch the relatively recent blockbuster Steven Spielberg cinematic version, **WAR OF THE WORLDS** (2005, USA), which this reviewer believes deals more with the original text's *tête-à-tête* between the author and the reader than any other adaptation to date. Taking the bold step of adapting the book still further, Timothy Hines' **WAR OF THE WORLDS: THE TRUE STORY** (2012, USA) incorporates authentic WWI newsreel footage with ingenious modern effects to produce a wry and rather accurate rendition (harking, in a way, back to Welles' radio play)—or "reboot", as is now popular to say—of Wells' original book, cleverly bypassing any reference to the 1953 cinematic—shall we say—"debacle" whatsoever.

Now, clearly, Pal's film should be given due credit for what it was: an ambitious and entertaining "state-of-the-art" special effects film for its time. In '53, science fiction cinema as we have come to know it today had just explosively evolved out of the primordial Hollywood ooze—had an abrupt "growth spurt", if you will—thus producing a sudden abundance of memorable and inventive films in a short span of time. Top honors for that year also go to William Cameron Menzies' **INVADERS FROM MARS**, Jack Arnold's **IT CAME FROM OUTER SPACE**, Eugène Lourié's **THE BEAST FROM 20,000 FATHOMS**, plus Arch Oboler's **THE TWONKY** and Terence Fisher's **FOUR SIDED TRIANGLE**, too.

Let's make it clear here, though: although I might most associate producer Geo. Pal with it when talking about **TWOTW**, and it may well have been his love of effects that made it what it is, it was, however, director Byron Haskin and his longtime love of science fiction which kept the film from turning into a complete shambles. Haskin, a special effects man before turning director, was also known for the proto ecological disaster movie **THE NAKED JUNGLE** (1954, USA; another Pal production), **ROBINSON CRUSOE ON MARS** (1964, USA; albeit *not* produced by his pal Pal this time, and, despite the awful title, not a bad film at all), and the telekinetic terror thriller **THE POWER** (1968, USA), as well as his work on the seminal '60s SF TV series *The Outer Limits* (1963-65 USA), which included my personal favorites "The Architects of Fear", "Behold Eck!" and "Demon With a Glass Hand"... (Okay, you get the point! Enough already!)

Top: The alien from *The Outer Limits* episode "The Architects of Fear". **Above:** A Martian from **THE WAR OF THE WORLDS** (1953)

Time to cut to the chase. The above template review features these standardized formatting requests:

FILM TITLES should be given in bold and uppercase, sans italics. To reiterate, when citing feature films or full-length documentaries, please use a bolded all-caps format: for example, **THE WAR OF THE WORLDS** (1953, USA).

Television Series Titles and *Book Titles*, plus such other things as *Stage Plays*, *Comic Books* or other periodicals (including *Magazines*, *Fanzines* and *Newspapers*), as well as *Record Albums* (etc.) should all be given in italics upper/lowercase, as applicable. To reiterate, when citing a TV series, please do so thusly: *The Outer Limits* (1963-65, USA). Individual episode titles, like short story titles or song titles (etc.), should be given in double quotes, sans italics (e.g., "The Architects of Fear").

"Foreign" words, phrases or titles should be italicized, as per the typical standard, with their proper special characters in place, if known (e.g., *Ä* or *é* or *ū* or *ç* [etc]).

Any internet references such as URL addresses should be italicized, without underlining.

Also, please take proper care to research your work beforehand to make sure all of your info is sound, and not just hearsay or—gods forbid—you figured you'd simply fabricate some "facts" just to spice things up some! But other than that, feel free to use whatever terminology you want (even cuss-words; we don't mind).

Now, we aren't expecting everyone to get *everything* perfect, by any means. But it would be totally awesome if you our valued contributors can at least get things as close to the ballpark as possible. Of course there are grey areas and any number of potential variables involved, but if you could at least kindly adhere to as many of the general guidelines given here as possible, we'll take care of the finishing touches. Thanking you in advance! ~**Tim P., Steve F., Tony S.** & **Brian H.**

"Oh, cool... monsters!!!"
~ Heather Paxton

EQUINOX

THE ROUNDTABLE

*"FAMED SCIENTIST DISAPPEARS... MASTER OF OCCULT MYSTERI-
OUSLY MISSING... What happened to Dr. Waterman? Only this man, last
to see him alive, knows...* **EQUINOX**! *The invisible barrier between good
and evil. The invisible barrier between light and the forces of darkness.
The supernatural, before your very eyes, as four teenage boys and girls
fight a devil cult for their sanity! For their lives! For their eternal souls!
...***EQUINOX***! A story that defies logic, confounds belief! ...What was the
secret of the thousand-year-old book? What are the unspeakable horrors
conjured by the forces of evil? What is the fiendish power of the ring that
enslaves and destroys? What is the one symbol that can hold at bay the
hosts of Hell unleashed on Earth? ...***EQUINOX***! Proving again that there
is more in Heaven and on Earth than is dreamt of in our philosophy!
...***EQUINOX***! [IN SUPERNATURAL COLOR] Begins where* **ROSE-
MARY'S BABY** *left off!"*

–Text blurbs and voiceover narration from Jack H. Harris' US theatrical trailer

Credits

Year: 1967

Running Time: 71 minutes

Director: Dennis Muren

Writer & Co-Director: Mark Thomas
McGee

Producer: Dennis Muren

Music: Truman Fisher

Cast: Skip Shimer, Barbara Hewitt,
Frank Bonner (as "Frank Boers, Jr."),
Robin Snider, Fritz Leiber

Credits

Year: 1970

Running Time: 82 minutes

Director & Writer: Jack Woods

Producer: Jack H. Harris

Music: John Caper

Cinematographer: Mike Hoover

Cast: Skip Shimer (as "Edward Connell"),
Barbara Hewitt, Frank Bonner (as "Frank
Boers, Jr."), Robin Snider (as "Robin
Christopher"), Fritz Leiber, Jack Woods

US one-sheet poster (art by Hughes)

A TALE OF TWO MONSTERS:
A LOOK AT *THE EQUINOX...A JOURNEY INTO THE SUPERNATURAL* (1967) and *EQUINOX* (1970)

by Christopher William Koenig

Look up the career of special effects artist Dennis Muren and you will find a plethora of titles to which he has contributed his talents: **STAR WARS** (1977), **E.T. THE EXTRA-TERRESTRIAL** (1982), **THE ABYSS** (1989) and **JURASSIC PARK** (1993, all USA), just to name a few. And yet, long before his Hollywood success, Muren did have his humble beginnings in the 1960s as a kid who liked science fiction and horror movies, admiring the stop-motion animation and visual effects of Ray Harryhausen and Willis O'Brien, and making his own amateur special effects shorts on 8mm and 16mm. His love of special effects and monster flicks would culminate with first foray into feature-length filmmaking, **THE EQUINOX...A JOURNEY INTO THE SUPERNATURAL**, which showcased Muren's know-how of providing special effects on a very low-budget. However, Muren needed help in achieving his vision and turned to fellow monster movie enthusiasts for assistance: novice

stop-motion animator and **KING KONG** '33 admirer David Allen to bring forth a monster or two and aspiring screenwriter Mark Thomas McGee to provide a script that would incorporate some semblance of a "story" to support the effects elements. Muren even went so far as getting professional visual effects artist Jim Danforth to provide a few matte paintings here and there.

Shot on 16mm between the years 1965-66 and finished in 1967, the film would eventually find a theatrical release in 1970 via producer Jack H. Harris as **EQUINOX**, a reedited version featuring additional material added by Jack Woods. Over the years, both versions have garnered interest from cult and monster movie fans, due to the original's behind-the-scenes origins as a project made by young monster movie enthusiasts, as well as becoming a popular staple of classic drive-in fare cheese. The **EQUINOX** version would have a healthy life being shown on television in the 1970s and released on home video in the 1980s (in two versions by Charlie Band's then Wizard Video: first as **EQUINOX** and later under the odd video-generated title **THE BEAST**), whereas the original **THE EQUINOX...A JOURNEY INTO THE SUPERNATURAL** would have some exposure on fuzzy bootleg videos in the mid-1990s. And who would've thought that the Criterion Collection would give this low-budget home movie/drive-in flick the grade-A DVD treatment in 2006, presenting both versions, which provide an interesting look into the differences between Muren's original edit and the more commonly seen theatrical release version.

THE EQUINOX...A JOURNEY INTO THE SUPERNATURAL opens with a fiery "*BANG!*" when an explosion occurs at an old cemetery out in the woods, knocking young teen Dave Fielding (Skip Shimer) to the ground. Dave gets up from the ground and sees the shadowy image of Death hovering over him, exclaiming to Dave, "You are cursed by all the forces of hell to die a year and a day from this moment". Running in fear, Dave approaches a bridge and tries to flag a car down for help. But, the car that approaches hits Dave, knocking him out; the car pulls to the side, revealing no driver inside it. Dave is eventually found and sent to a hospital to recover. A year passes and a reporter arrives at the hospital to see that Dave has been placed in isolation; when the reporter shows a picture of college teacher Dr. Waterman (Fritz Leiber) to Dave, he panics and attacks the reporter. After the reporter is taken out of the isolation room, the doctor plays a tape recording of Dave telling his story when he first arrived: Dave had received a call from

Dr. Waterman, asking for Dave to drop by for a visit in his cabin in the woods. Along with his friend Jim (Frank Bonner), his girlfriend Vicki (Robin Snider), and Dave's blind-date Susan (Barbara Hewitt), the four teens head out to the woods and discover the professor's cabin has been completely destroyed. The teens wander about and spy an ancient castle off in the distance. As they attempt to get closer to this castle, they hear the sound of evil laughter coming from a cave and find a crazy hermit inside who gives the group an old book. As Dave tries to examine the book, Dr. Waterman suddenly appears and tries to steal it, but Dave and Jim tackle him down, whereupon Waterman dies immediately thereafter. Dave and Jim walk away from the professor's corpse for a moment, but upon their return...Waterman's body has disappeared! Things get stranger when the castle also disappears; Dave and Jim discover the castle is trapped behind an "invisible barrier", making it appear/disappear at certain intervals. But things get even weirder when the kids are attacked by various giant monsters, such as a giant ape-like creature and a large green-skinned demon. Discovering a note written by Dr. Waterman in the book, the note mentions that the book contains secret passages which opened an alternate dimension of Hell, and the various creatures the teens have encountered are trying to get the book back for their master, the Devil!

Considering **THE EQUINOX...A JOURNEY INTO THE SUPERNATURAL** was two years in the making for both its director Dennis Muren and writer/co-director Mark Thomas McGee, it has to be understood that they were basically learning the filmmaking process during production, as, when looking at the final results, their experiences in directing actors and understanding story pacing were obviously only limited at best. A major problem with the film is McGee's script; it's fairly unstructured and it takes quite a bit of running time for the story to get moving as we are

Right: EQUINOX pics *[from top to bottom]* – Jim Danforth's stunning matte painting of the hilltop castle; the cadaver in the cave; a hellish skeletal imp, seen only in the '67 cut of the film; and him (it?) dubbed "Taurus" by animator David Allen, creator of said stop-motion anthropoid monstrosity and the film's other animated creatures

presented with undeveloped characters who recite meaningless dialogue while wandering around in the woods. While the script does have some interesting ideas here and there (the set-up of four teens battling monsters and Satan in the woods is a perfect hook in itself), the storyline has too many gaps in logic. Take the scene in which the teens confront the old man in the cave: the nutty hermit tells them the "demons" won't get the book from him, and then in no less than a second the man proceeds to give the confused kids the book with no qualms whatsoever! Another weak link in the original cut is that the acting is fairly dull: with the slight exception of Frank Bonner, who makes do with his one-dimensional character (and, out of the majority of the cast, Bonner would manage to go on and have a fairly healthy career on television and play the character Herb Tarlek in *WKRP in Cincinnati* [1978-82, USA]), the main cast is stuck playing bland characters and reciting go-nowhere dialogue, serving only as filler to build up the monster action. At best, Muren's only upside to the production is that he managed to present a decent grasp of technical proficiency in regards to camera set-ups, reaction shots, and blocking in order to make the film visually interesting. Also, Muren was able to provide his shoestring production with its own music score composed by Pasadena City College professor Truman Fisher, which is quite good and helps complement the film's more exciting moments, though occasionally Fisher utilizes the Theremin sound effects a little too much in some spots.

But, the scrappy plotting and so-so acting are just filler; the main goal of **THE EQUINOX...A JOURNEY INTO THE SUPERNATURAL** is to unleash the various monsters, matte-paintings, and clever optical effects which Muren and his team can muster on a piecemeal budget. David Allen provides his stop-motion talents to bring to life such creations as a giant Cephalopod-squid that, in an all-too-brief scene, destroys the doctor's cabin, and a King Kong-inspired ape-like monster (dubbed "Taurus" by Allen) which chases the teens; while Dennis Muren introduces the Devil—complete with wings, a trident tail, and claw-like feet—with decent results. Muren also provides an impressive live-action effects sequence featuring a giant green-colored monster, with a mutant face and dressed in prehistoric garb, chasing one of the teens for the book: the entire effect is nicely realized by forced perspective cinematography done in-camera, with no usage of split-screens or optical processing. Shots of the mysterious castle are provided by Jim Danforth via the usage of glass matte paintings, and they are quite breathtaking (almost too good for this production, I'll say).

But, whereas **THE EQUINOX...A JOURNEY INTO THE SUPERNATURAL** is more-or-less a glorified home movie, the final release version **EQUINOX** is an attempt at polishing and improving the original's technical issues and expanding its storyline just a bit. Despite the original cut being finished in 1967, Dennis Muren found that very few distributors were interested in releasing his homemade production. However, independent distributor/producer Jack H. Harris saw possibilities in Muren's film. Harris was no stranger to being involved with special effects productions: his first independently produced film, directed by Irvin S. Yeaworth, Jr., was **THE BLOB** (1958, USA), which would help introduce Steve McQueen on the screen, featured some effective sequences involving the title outer space menace attacking people, realized via melted silicon and miniature set hydraulics; **4D MAN** (1959, USA) displayed clever matte effects and optical cinematography to present its actor Robert Lansing walking thru walls; **DINOSAURUS!** (1960, USA) would feature a stop-motion animated Tyrannosaurus Rex and Brontosaurus, both revived via lightning, threatening the lives of construction workers and villagers on an island off St. Croix. Muren's film was a shoe-in for distribution, but Harris could see the film needed some work and brought in film editor/sound editor Jack Woods, who had worked on doctoring some Roger Corman productions and serving postproduction on John Cassavetes' films **FACES** (1968) and **HUSBANDS** (1970, both USA), to reedit the film, as well as write and direct new material (Dennis Muren would be credited as "associate producer" and Mark Thomas McGee is credited for providing the original story), while Harris would shorten the film's title to simply **EQUINOX**.

In the **EQUINOX** version, Woods basically sticks with the original narrative structure as used in Muren's original cut. However, Woods expands the story further by exploring more about the origins and the meanings behind the mysterious book, as well as providing the added bonus of including another character: a shifty forest ranger named Asmodeus (played by Woods himself), who turns out to be the Devil in human disguise and has taken possession over Susan. It has to be said that the addition of Asmodeus is a bit of a mixed bag: on the one hand, Asmodeus does present a more direct antagonist for the main characters to interact with, as opposed to just having various monsters hound the cast with little rhyme or reason like the original cut did; yet on the other side, the idea that the Devil would go about in disguise as a forest ranger using the ancient name "Asmodeus" does illicit a chuckle or two (it's even more silly when, later on, Dave realizes that Asmodeus is the nickname for the Devil; how did Dave just happen to figure that out all of a sudden?). The added material featuring the original cast can occasionally be

obvious, especially when you can see things like Frank Bonner's sideburns alternating between short in the original footage and long in the new sequences, or that Skip Shimer's hairstyle keeps alternating back and forth between the old and new material, but it's not intrusive nor do any of the added scenes come off as padding; rather, Woods takes advantage of these new scenes to expand the one-dimensional characters and flesh out the original's limited storyline. Another benefit **EQUINOX** has over its original version is better film editing and a very robust sound effects track, as Woods adds some polish and finesse in his version, tightening shots and effects scenes with a better sense of pacing. Woods substituted the original Truman Fisher score with a plethora of stock music supplied by John Caper; most of the scores originate from Jaime Mendoza-Nava, and those familiar cues can also be heard in William O. Brown's **THE WITCHMAKER** (1969, USA). However, Woods uses the cues to the extent that the film has wall-to-wall scoring in every frame—which comes off as very unnecessary in some parts—as opposed to Muren's cut, which used Fisher's original score very sparingly.

Despite the attempts at improving the original's technical limitations, **EQUINOX** takes away the rough-and-ready, do-it-yourself home movie

The simian henchbeast from the so-called "equinox between worlds" puts paid to the crazy old man from the cave. Thankfully seen plenty in both versions of **EQUINOX** and known (if not in the actual films themselves) as "Taurus", in the '70 edit the all-new Asmodeus character describes it as being a "30-foot ape"; although it is clearly nowhere near *that* tall

13

1980 UK VHS cover (artist's name illegible)

vibe present in **THE EQUINOX...A JOURNEY INTO THE SUPERNATURAL**. Dennis Muren's original version has a slight charm to it that can be appreciated if one is willing to see the enthusiasm amongst the flaws. Yet, on the other side of the coin, Jack Woods and Jack H. Harris managed to take a flawed production and made serviceable improvements to the story and onscreen action. In all honesty, both cuts have their ups and downs, their pros and cons. For me, personall , it's a toss-up: I find enjoyment in either version, as both cuts provide prime cheesy monster movie madness. And really, that's all we monster-movie lovers can expect from either version, and we're certainly better off for it.

EQUINOX: A STORY THAT DEFIES LOGIC

by Michael Hauss

I remember seeing **EQUINOX**—or **THE BEAST**, as it was called back in the mid-'80s—on VHS from Wizard video, and upon viewing it I knew I was entering into the world of low-budget nirvana. This little monster movie, in my eyes, while flawed, spoke to that amateur filmmaker in me; the one who always said I could do that better, the one who never did but lived the dream of a fanciful,

youthful belief in artistic creation. I watched the film repeatedly, always finding more to enjoy and things to keep sparking my imagination. I watched scenes that struggle to make sense, but I also looked at the sheer determination of the filmmakers in each scene to create something from nothing. I imagined the cast and crew lobbying for funds from many sources to get this film made, maybe going deeply in debt to do so. In my mind, the film always tried hard, and to me trying hard meant something and spoke to my monster-loving heart.

I became obsessed with this film, and I told my friends and recommended it to them wholeheartedly, but after viewing it they thought I was quite insane or stupid, or both in some cases. So, within my ever-shrinking group of friends I was the champion of this "piece of sh*t", as my friend Bill—the guy who put cigarettes out on his arm—called it. I came out of the '80s and '90s with nothing more than a few awkward photos of the long beautiful mullet that adorned my head and this tattered Wizard video VHS tape. I was amazed when I saw that **EQUINOX** had been released in the Criterion Collection. I knew that my belief in this film had been validated and hurried after receiving it in the mail to visit Bill who, oddly enough, works in a tobacco store. Bill was, in his normal dour mood, almost Steven Wright-like, but even more sarcastic and less philosophical in his profanity-laced retorts. So, when I stood in front of Bill—who is my only friend left from my mullet days—and held up my validation, he eyes the monster on the cover and the light goes on, and, you know what he says? "*My God!* They released that piece of sh*t on DVD?!" I felt like a scorned child, and tried to come back with a witty reply, but I could not think of a thing. Scorn turned to anger then I rushed out of the store and decided to delete him from my Facebook friends. I rushed home, held the DVD in my trembling hands, and knew regardless of the outcome of this viewing that I was holding a piece of my cinematic viewing history before me.

I inserted the DVD and waited for the start; I know what people say about this film and the continuity issues of trying to piece a film together after a lapse of years in the start and completion of it. **EQUINOX** works hard to incorporate many horror elements, and some of the effects and monsters are good considering the low budget and technical limitations of the production. I sat down and watched the film, and after the movie had completed I went over to my computer and sent a Facebook friend request to Bill, he had been right after all these years. It was as bad as he said. I was thrown into a depression for many days until I came to realize one thing: this film, like my mullet, was *never* good.

Many days after the viewing I was still in a bit of a funk over this film, until I sat one cold snowy night and looked out the window, and the flood of memories associated with my love of **EQUINOX** and monsters made me understand something about myself. I then knew that my film viewing was never a public event and that my pressing for people to enjoy my love of this film made me view it from a critical eye rather than as a fan of the horror genre. I waited months before I tried to view it again, and, you know what? The love for this little monster movie came back into my heart. Like the Grinch when he understands the true meaning of Christmas, I again knew that the meaning of film is the love we feel inside for it, not the critical reaction it or we receive. The fanciful belief in artistic creation may waver with age and time, but the dream never completely dies.

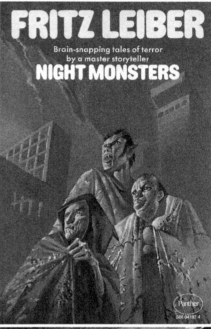

THE STRANGE CASE OF DR. WATERMAN

by Mike T. Lyddon

In the story of **THE EQUINOX...A JOURNEY INTO THE SUPERNATURAL**, four young people go in search of the elusive geologist Dr. Arthur Waterman, only to find interdimensional terror beyond their wildest imaginations. One might not give a second thought about the character's brief appearance in the film, but it is legendary fantastic fiction author Fritz Leiber (Jr.)'s role as Waterman which reveals some stunning correlations between the movie and Lovecraft's Cthulhu Mythos... if only by sheer accident!

It's no secret that Forrest J. Ackerman, the man behind *Famous Monsters* magazine and a keystone in American horror and science fiction for decades, helped Dennis Muren and company with various aspects of **EQUINOX**, including some of the casting.

It was Ackerman who brought in Fritz Leiber (1910-1992) to play the small yet key role of Dr. Waterman, a man whose obsession with "the book" did not end well for the aging geologist. Ackerman apparently saw Leiber as another potential movie monster icon like Vincent Price or Christopher Lee, but unfortunately Leiber's screen résumé never added up to more than a handful of movies. It's interesting to note that Leiber's father Fritz Leiber, Sr. (1882-1949), with whom he shared a rather strong familial resemblance, was a Shakespearean-trained stage actor who got his start in silent films playing Mercutio in a 1916 adaptation of **ROMEO AND JULIET**. As well as appearing in some more silent films, Fritz, Sr. later landed small, frequently uncredited supporting roles in numerous Hollywood "talkies": for example, as an elderly aristocrat in William Dieterle's **THE HUNCHBACK OF NOTRE DAME** (1939), starring Charles Laughton as Quasimodo;

Top: Fritz Leiber, Jr., as he is first seen in the film, as a photograph in a dossier. **Center:** Illustrator Bruce Pennington's cover to Panther Books' 1975 British paperback edition of one of the usual author and occasional actor's short story collections (the collection had previously been issued in the US in 1969—albeit with less stories—in an Ace "Double" edition, with different cover art by Jack Gaughan). **Above:** Leiber as Dr. Waterman checks out in **EQUINOX**

15

Leiber's first published collection from 1947
(cover art by Ronald Clyne)

as composer Franz Liszt in Arthur Lubin's **PHAN-TOM OF THE OPERA** (1943), starring Claude Rains in the title role; as Dr. Charles Morris in Henry Levin's Lewtonesque lycanthropy tale **CRY OF THE WEREWOLF** (1944), and as a man of the cloth in Julien Duvivier's war drama **THE IM-POSTOR** (a.k.a. **STRANGE CONFESSION**) that same year. His last onscreen acting appearance was as Mr. Poole in the Anthony Mann Western **DEV-IL'S DOORWAY** (1950).

"So, *who* is Fritz Leiber?" (Jr.), you might well ask. This is where things get really interesting. Keep in mind that Leiber had nothing to do with the writing

of **EQUINOX**, he was merely hired as an actor in the film.

In the mid-1930s, Fritz Leiber, Jr. was a young, aspiring writer looking for that big spark of inspiration. He decided to write a letter to his literary hero Howard Phillips Lovecraft, and of course Mr. Lovecraft responded with great words of encouragement for the budding author. This was a defining moment for Leiber, who took those positive vibes and went on to become one of the most important genre writers of the latter half of the 20th Century.

Winner of multiple Hugo and Nebula awards for his remarkable works of fiction, including the acclaimed novel *The Wanderer* (1964), about a nomadic planet that wreaks havoc when it enters the Earth's solar system, as well as *A Specter is Haunting Texas* (1969), about a future where cowboy-lovin' good ol' boys take over the United States, and such brilliant short stories as "Gonna Roll the Bones", which first appeared in Harlan Ellison's groundbreaking speculative fiction anthology *Dangerous Visions* (1967), all the way to his extensive sword-and-sorcery series featuring *Fafhrd and the Gray Mouser*, which spanned more than 50 years, Leiber's earliest work was based largely upon Lovecraft's Cthulhu Mythos, and one can find some of these stories in Leiber's first published collection of tales, entitled *Night's Black Agents* (Arkham House, 1947). It is here that his coincidental connection to **EQUINOX** is the strongest.

There are a few aspects to both the Cthulhu Mythos and **EQUINOX** which bear more than just a passing resemblance. For starters, we have an ancient book of evil (In Lovecraft's universe, *The Necronomicon*) that opens interdimensional doorways allowing a variety of nasty creatures and deities to pass through. Then there are the characters who be-

Fritz Leiber as Dr. Waterman peruses "the book", and it proves to be quite the page-turner, if not exactly light reading

Tome Of Terror: Bruce Campbell as Ash, with *The Necronomicon* in **THE EVIL DEAD** (1981, USA)

come possessed by the book in order to do its bidding while others battle (usually in vain) to break its spells.

One can only imagine Leiber's reaction to reading the script as one of perhaps *"Hmmm... I've seen this somewhere before!"* Indeed, his role of Dr. Waterman could be interchanged with any number of characters from either his or Lovecraft's mythos stories, which makes his short-but-sweet part in **EQUINOX** one of either divine intervention or simple cosmic coincidence. It should be noted that Mark McGee, who penned the original **EQUINOX** story, never read any of Lovecraft's stories (!), and said he was instead inspired by Jacques Tourneur's classic horror film **NIGHT OF THE DEMON** (1957, UK), which was released in the US as **CURSE OF THE DEMON**.

Perhaps it was the diabolic genius of Forry Ackerman which manipulated this unholy union of Leiber and **EQUINOX** in a master stroke of cinematic legerdemain! After all, he was friends with Leiber for many years, and he certainly knew what Dennis Muren's monster movie entailed.

Sadly, when Jack H. Harris picked up **THE EQUI-NOX...A JOURNEY INTO THE SUPERNAT-URAL** and reedited it for distribution a few years later as **EQUINOX**, he decided to leave out some of Dr. Waterman's explanatory scenes about "the book", which are uncannily similar to scenes in Sam Raimi's **THE EVIL DEAD** (1981, USA), a film that would be written and produced more than a decade later. It should be noted that in **THE EVIL DEAD**, the book is even directly referred to as *The Necronomicon*.

Fritz Leiber's own stories enjoyed some success adapted to both the silver screen and television. His original novel *Conjure Wife* (1943) was adapted four times, most famously as **NIGHT OF THE EAGLE** (a.k.a. **BURN, WITCH, BURN!**, 1962, UK), whose screenplay was written by no less than *Twilight Zone*'s magic man Charles Beaumont along with another *TZ* alumni and master storyteller Richard Matheson, famous for such sci-fi/horror novels as *The Shrinking Man* and *I Am Legend* (see *Monster!* #13, pp.64-80).

Leiber's short story "The Girl with the Hungry Eyes" (1949)—about a psychic vampire—was adapted twice, the last time in 1995 for a feature film of the same name directed by Jon Jacobs, but originally as an episode of Rod Serling's *Night Gallery*. Leiber also had another story called "The Dead Man" adapted for that series, Serling's short-lived follow-up to *The Twilight Zone*.

While Leiber's performance as Dr. Waterman in both incarnations of **EQUINOX** is probably seen by most "film historians" as a trivial footnote at best, for me it represents one of those strange and wonderfully intangible moments in horror film history where the planets were in their proper alignment, and perhaps we will never know who—or *what*—was pulling the proverbial strings...

NOTE: See also
http://en.wikipedia.org/wiki/Fritz_Leiber
http://asitecalledfred.com/2006/07/06/noctur-nal-admissions-dvd-review-equinox/
http://www.criterion.com/films/780-equinox
http://www.criterion.com/current/posts/2467-books-of-the-dead

PREACHING TO THE CONVERTED:
AN AFFECTIONATE AND FAR FROM UNBIASED (RE)APPRAISAL OF *EQUINOX*

by Steve Fenton

The striking US half-sheet poster (art by Hughes?)

I had my first fateful encounter with this perennial personal favorite—which is as much-maligned by many as it is dearly beloved by many others—back in around 1982 or '83 or thereabouts, when I first taped it off late-night Canadian TV (on my parents' clunking great top-loading Sony Betamax VCR, of all things!), and I've had a warm and squishy soft spot for it in both my heart and head ever since. So my defensive/protective kneejerk reaction to any naysayer asking me what I see in such a low-budget, often amateurish and rough-around-the-edges cinematic exercise would be a hearty, unabashed and unconditional *"What's NOT to like?!"* Sure, it's one of those "nostalgic" items which I was initially exposed to as a much younger man, and, as so often happens, we tend to harbor fonder memories for things first experienced in our youth simply because we are re-viewing them via not just the reversed, perception-warping/enhancing telescope of hazy hindsight but also through the rose-colored glasses of our more youthful idealism, which (speaking for myself) often becomes tainted and eroded with the accumulation of years—make that whole *decades*— and, I'm sad to say, today **EQUINOX** doesn't move

me in quite the same wonderful way(s) as it did when I was a much more naïvely idealistic fellow in my early twenties. But such is life. Perhaps, now that I've become so much more hardened ("seasoned"?) by all my extra accumulated years and additional life experience I am now somehow incapable of re-experiencing it as I initially did, but that's by no means to imply that I don't still derive a great deal of pleasure from the film whenever I revisit it, and I most definitely do regard it as cozy "comfort" viewing of the highest order, from which I typically derive some new small and heretofore overlooked pleasure each time I re-see it.

But, believe it or not, although I'm a longtime fan of Jack H. Harris' added-to/subtracted-from recut of **EQUINOX**, until recently—specifically for this special *Monster!* "roundtable" this very month, as a matter of fact—I hadn't ever watched producer/director Dennis Muren's and writer/co-director Mark Thomas McGee's original unaltered (some might say unadulterated) 1967 cut, the comparatively cumbersomely-titled **THE EQUINOX...A JOURNEY INTO THE SUPERNATURAL**; but over the past

30-odd (hell, going on *40*!) years I have seen Harris' 1970 "modification" upwards of a dozen (probably around fifteen) times, and that's a lot for me, because there are only comparatively few movies which I ever re-watch anywhere near that often (I have a long list of such super-faves, but that's neither here nor there in the present context, so I'll refrain from reeling off any titles).

Anyway, having at long last watched the cruder, more no-frills '67 precursor to the more honed and cohesive '70 reedit, I must say I enjoyed the former just fine; yet, without the smarmily sinister, face-pulling Asmodeus to help tie things together better and give us a more palpable central villain to hiss at, the film has a lot less character as well as coherence, for my money. Undeniably—and no, I'm not just saying this because it's the version I'm most used to; I'm speaking objectively, as I see it—Harris' modification for the most part gels far more effectively than Muren/McGee's forerunner does. That former version (in actuality the latter, chronologically speaking!) is just so much better fleshed-out plot-wise, and overall more stylishly constructed, too. That said, however, there are a few scenes in the '67 edit that I think should have made it into the '70 one, although, thinking objectively, I can kind of understand why they didn't make the cut (e.g., those stop-motion trident-toting skeletal devils glimpsed in the earlier edit but not in the later one might well be considered a tad too cutely puppet-like for most viewers, and would likely provoke chuckles of derision [albeit not from me... *never!*]). Also, the sometimes (okay, *often*times) wildly out-of-synch dialogue, which is most apparent in **E** '67, but still evident in sections of **E** '70, only adds to the cumulative otherworldliness; there are scenes which literally appear to have come from some crudely post-synched Euro or other overdubbed foreign import. Having watched so many often poorly-dubbed movies in my time, though, the fact that the words don't always even remotely fit the movements of actors' lips is a mere piddling consideration which doesn't distract or detract from my enjoyment one iota, and it merely reinforces the overall off-balance, alien ambience still further.

In regards to **EQUINOX**'s seemingly long-lasting influence, as the reminiscences/ruminations of some of our other contributors this ish so well attest, it certainly wasn't just myself who was lastingly affected by it. It's a pretty safe bet to assume—as many people have assumed over the years—that Sam Raimi took more than a few pointers from the film's base premise/milieu for use in **THE EVIL DEAD**, as there are just too many more than only passing similarities for it to have been mere coincidence (as well, Don Coscarelli's fantabulous **PHANTASM** seemingly owes its share of debts to **EQUINOX**, and many other films have been either directly or indirectly influenced by it over the years... whether

Herb Tarlek Goes To The Devil? During a sequence seen only in the '67 cut of the film, Frank Bonner as the Jim character (actually only his diabolic *doppelgänger*) undergoes a startling transformation c/o a crude double-exposure effect into...well, you know

EQUINOX '70 co-director/co-star Jack Woods laughs it up as Asmodeus. Being an arrogant a-hole is about the *least* of his bad qualities, however!

they know it [or would admit to it] or not. Also, although I haven't seen it in a goodly number of years so cannot say with any certitude, I'm pretty sure it was an at least partial influence on John "Bud" Cardos' charming lo-budge sto-mo sci-fantasy **THE DAY TIME ENDED** [1979, USA], too.[1] Indeed, a comprehensive list of all the films influenced by **EQUINOX** would sure take some compiling, I reckon. In fact, it'd be a damned near *impossible* feat to accomplish).

On the downside (if only a minor gripe), one of the more dubious aspects of both versions of the film are their blatant advertisements for unrelated, "incidental" consumer products. Namely the rather in-your-face product placements for the then-still-relatively-new-fangled Polaroid camera and KFC fast food back when it was more formally known as Kentucky Fried Chicken (i.e., their pre-wingless, beakless and featherless genetically engineered mutant poultry era, when it actually still had real chicken in it! ☺). Although its brand-name is never really made apparent either visually or vocally, said instant camera is repeatedly on view as a prop in both versions of the film. The much more brazen KFC spot ("Saved by the Colonel!" enthuses Frank Bonner's peckish character at the woodland picnic) is seen only in **EQUINOX** '70, during which a party-size bucket emblazoned with the Col. Sanders logo is placed front and center-screen, actually—*for shame!*—receiving more screen-time than that wonderful tentacular / cephalopodic monstrosity so fleetingly seen elsewhere dismantling Dr. Waterman's country digs. In the original cut of the film, only a pile of discarded freshly-gnawed chicken bones are seen in C/U during the "kids'" picnic, *sans* any built-in ad-spot.

While hard-sell commercial placements are unfortunately still very much with us today (and then some!), other more dated aspects of the film now appear quaintly archaic, which only adds to the fun all the more (come to think of it, I'm pretty sure they would have appeared outdated to me back in the early '80s too, even naïve as I was then). For instance, some of the social interaction between members of the opposite sexes within the narrative (mainly Bonner's mildly chauvinistic Jim character and his docile doormat girlfriend Vicki [played by buxom blonde Robin Christopher], who certainly doesn't seem to be much of a Women's Libber). **EQUINOX** originates from back in those pre-PC days—long before the battle of the sexes turned into all-out war—when a guy could casually call his GF stupid or tell her to "dummy-up" in front of their friends and still expect her to make the sandwiches and coffee, and she'd scream her head off then trip over and fall flat on her face while attempting to run away from a monster, taking everything in stride as a matter of course in her clearly delineated role as damsel-in-distress. All kidding aside though, most of the films' (note plural) halfhearted attempts at "humanizing" their protagonists via "realistic" banter and whatnot largely fall flat thanks to wooden acting and unconvincing dialogue; but then, monster movies have typically not been known for their pinpoint accuracy when it comes to the complexities of interrelations between their more human characters anyway, so it isn't like it's anything out of the ordinary for the genre, unlike thankfully many of **EQUINOX**'s other less-mundane aspects.

Speaking of which, for whatever unfathomable reasons known only to them, some people object to the fabulous character of Mr. Asmodeus (actually *you-know-who* in earthly guise, charismatically played by Jack Woods, who also directed the new insert scenes for the '70 version) as being too incongruous, even outright ridiculous. But I respectfully beg to differ. Seen wearing a cowboy hat in uniform while sat astride a horse in many of his scenes, this phony-baloney-as-hell forest ranger character acts openly mockingly scornful and menacing towards our heroes, but nobody seems to notice his sinisterly surly, snarly demeanor towards them, despite the obviousness of his freely announced handle (which, in a daffy delayed reaction, the group's supposedly most "quick-witted" member David [the top-billed "Skip Shimer"/Edward Connell, in his only known film role] later clues into from out of nowhere). The scene wherein the suitably assholish (and *worse*) Asmodeus corners the main heroine Susan (winsomely willowy blonde Barbara Hewitt) alone in the woods and attempts to (*ahem*) "seduce" her—both figuratively and literally drooling all down himself, and very nearly onto the camera lens as well in the process—still possesses a perversely unsettling tone. An all-new addition seen only in the '70 reedit, as is Woods/Asmodeus himself, said far-less-graphic

[1] **EQUINOX**'s David Allen and Jim Danforth were among the numerous visual effects technicians who worked on the film

scene here was seemingly part-inspired by the notorious "devil rape" of Mia Farrow in Polanski's masterful **ROSEMARY'S BABY** (1968, USA); a likelihood which seems all the more probable due to the simple fact that said occult blockbuster was tactically name-dropped right in Jack H. Harris' first-run US theatrical trailer for **EQUINOX** '70. While he's slobbering all over her—he *is* the damn Devil, after all; it's what he does!—Asmodeus unwittingly uncovers not only sexy Susan's trim midriff but her concealed silver Christian cross too, an accidental exposure which promptly causes him to beat a hasty retreat while mugging all the more grotesquely still at the camera in distorted foreshortened close-ups which almost appear to have been shot with a fish-eye lens (to me he resembles some outrageous caricature of George Clooney in these shots!). In my opinion—which is what all this stuff I'm saying here is, needless to say—his freakish glowering and grimacing tightrope-walks that fragile fine line between unsettlingly grotesque and goofily foolish without actually straying too far in the latter direction so that it becomes outright laughable. For me, all his malevolent peering, leering and sneering merely serve to make the character that much more memorable—dare I say near-as-dammit to Walter Huston as ol' Mr. Scratch in William Dieterle's **ALL THAT MONEY CAN BUY** (a.k.a. **THE DEVIL AND DANIEL WEBSTER**, 1941, USA [yet another Criterion disc release, incidentally])?—and whenever I re-view the present film I always look forward to Asmodeus' scenes much more than I do most of the generally stiltedly acted stuff involving the protagonists (quite frankly, in some ways I find the flubber-faced Herb Tarlek's—sorry, I mean Frank Bonner's—apparently unintentional [?] mugging a lot more laughable than Woods' is! Although, that said, *WKRP*'s future resident loveable doorknob Bonner's odd facial expressions and disjointed acting style also strangely complement **EQUINOX**'s screwy looniverse in their own way, so I wouldn't want anyone else but him in the role, either. Way to go, Herb... *er*, Frank!).

But let's hear it for Mr. Asmodeus too! As of this writing, from what I've seen of *M!* #14's other contributions on the current general subject, I'm about the only one of us who seems to have much positive to say about the guy. I'll say again as I said above, "*What's NOT to like?!*"

While uttering loaded lines like "*Monster?* Well, there useta be a few brown bears around here, and maybe an occasional mountain lion, but I'm afraid we're fresh outta monsters" with a tongue-in-cheek, sarky smirk, along with his self-consciously sinis-

One of **EQUINOX**'s most Lovecraftian inclusions is this colossal tentacled abomination—of a supernatural cephalopod-like species which resembles a cross between an octopus and a shell-less chambered nautilus—which materializes to trash Dr. Waterman's isolated rural residence (with him in it!). Unfortunately, this marvelous monstrosity is only seen in but a single brief scene

During the exciting climax of **EQUINOX**, now having assumed his true form as a winged scarlet demon, the airborne Asmodeus swoops down hawk-like upon the fleeing David (Edward Connell) and Susan (Barbara Hewitt), only to be repelled by the large cruciform gravestone standing between it and them

ter aura and exaggeratedly twisted leers and sneers, I totally think Asmodeus perfectly fits the bizarre, off-kilter alternate reality of the film. I'll even go so far as to loudly and proudly proclaim here and now that he is my *absolute favorite* ("human" [note quotes]) character in the movie. (There, I said it! My reputation—such as it is—is well and truly shot now. Don't all pelt me with rotten veggies at once.) Consequently, to me, while Muren's, David Allen's and Jim Danforth's jim-dandy effects are indubitably the stars of the show in the truest sense, taking away Woods' "extraneous" tacked-on footage would be tantamount—just for example, off the top of my head—to snipping out all of super-ham Billy Thurman's pricelessly over-the-top crazy redneck scenes from Larry Buchanan's **IT'S ALIVE!** (1969, USA); that is to say, a far lesser film than it is. Come to think of it, that Buchanan film would be virtually *nothing* without Thurman's demented presence! Although, as **EQUINOX**'s '67 "thumbnail" version attests, the film is still more than tolerably watchable enough minus Woods' inclusion, as he is by no means absolutely crucial to its overall success, but he definitely does contribute to it in a major way. Of course, if I'd never seen him in the '70 cut umpteen times beforehand I wouldn't know what I was missing; because you can't miss what you've never had, and all that. However, since I *have*, I wouldn't want things any other way, but it's great to have both variations of the movie anyway, make no mistake about

it. I found watching the original a most rewarding belated experience indeed, and it has improved my appreciation for the alternate edition all the more.

In summation, when it comes to either/or **THE EQUINOX...A JOURNEY INTO THE SUPERNATURAL** and **EQUINOX**, rather than compare apples and oranges I'd much rather just have my cake and eat it too; so I'm more than happy to take *both*, thanks. The more the merrier, as far as I'm concerned!

"DON'T TELL ME WHAT I DIDN'T SEE!"
A Brief Meditation on *Equinox*

by John Szpunar

My earliest memories of watching **EQUINOX** are pretty hazy. I really can't remember how old I was when I first saw the thing. Come to think of it, I can't even remember where I was when I saw it. It's a strange feeling—for the most part, my childhood memories hover around the borders of total recall. This particular memory seems more like a dream. I don't have much to hold onto. All I can say is that I must have been very, very young.

22

I *do* remember one of those old TV sets from the '70s—the kind of thing that looks like the gut-buster from **VIDEODROME**. I remember the smell of Pine-Sol and Pledge. That probably would have placed me at my grandmother's house. It was dark outside—of that much I'm certain. I have a vague recollection of looking down at a brown and red rag rug—the kind of thing that a grandmother might have on her living room floor.

The TV was on, that's for sure. I remember seeing a car driving around with no one at the wheel. I remember a skeleton, a book, and a lot of frightening creatures. I remember seeing a weird green giant that looked like the guy on the cans of green beans in my mother's pantry. Yes, the TV was on, but I had no idea what I was watching.

Every now and then, I'd try to describe a few of these scenes to my friends at school. They'd walk away with confused expressions on their faces. I know it sounds like a cliché, but I often wondered if that strange movie had been some kind of dream.

The years went on, and I kind of forgot about the thing. And then, one afternoon at a friend's house: A skeleton, a book, and a lot of frightening creatures. Off-kilter camera angles and disembodied voices. *Well, holy shit!* Dr. Waterman, you old buzzard! How the hell have you been?

We had rented a tape called **THE BEAST**. At the time, I didn't know that thing was a Wizard Video retitling of **EQUINOX**. I wasn't even aware that there had been a name change. No matter, that. As the movie unfolded, a lot of lost memories came flooding back.

Now, let me put things into perspective. By this time I was no stranger to the...well, *stranger* side of cinema. Granted, I was still grappling with the medium's syntax. But after a steady diet of Saturday afternoon creature features, I knew that this film was completely different than the usual fare. In a way, it reminded me of listening to my Wade Denning Halloween records—a lot of off-camera dialogue, a lot of bargain-basement sound effects, and a lot of weird music. The actors looked like Dave Berg drawings from one of my dad's old issues of *Mad*. Hell, the entire thing looked like one of my grandfather's home movies.

That didn't matter to me. In fact, it only added to the film's strange charm. The stop-motion effects were rude and crude, but *damn* they were cool. In fact, they looked like something that my friends and I might be able to pull off.

My dad was still shooting Super 8 home movies at this point in time, so I asked him if I could borrow his camera. Unfortunately, he wouldn't let me anywhere near the thing. He told me that I'd most likely break it. I was pissed, but in retrospect, he was probably right. What I *did* gain access to was the family tape recorder. My brother and I would spend hours cackling into the microphone, creating our own weird stories complete with music and sound effects from my dad's old records.

What I'm getting at is this: seeing **EQUINOX** at that moment in time was a *major* flashpoint for me. The film singlehandedly made me look at movies in a way that I hadn't before. It was a trumpet call to action. It sparked my imagination and made me want to do something.

Top: Special effects wizard Dennis Muren poses out front of a theatre in 1970.
Above: The 1985 US "big box" VHS release of **EQUINOX**, under an alternate title (art unsigned)

Accomplished using a clever in-camera effect which utilized forced perspective to create the optical illusion (note that "miniature" tree in the foreground, providing scale), Jim Duron as the not-so-jolly green giant pursues Frank Bonner as Jim

I eventually did get a hold of a Super 8 camera, and man—I had a blast with it. I joined the Detroit Filmmakers Coalition with a few of my friends, and we were granted access to a 16mm Ari S. Sweet! We were shooting with the same kind of camera that Sam Raimi, Peter Jackson, and the guys from **EQUINOX** used! I can't say that any of our little movies ever held a candle to theirs, but that didn't matter. What *did* matter was the joy that we got from the entire process.

Which brings me back to **EQUINOX**.

The other day, a friend of mine asked me why I was so obsessed with what he called "bad" movies. "Why do you always go for the schlocky shit, Szpunar?" Well, there are way too many reasons to even start counting, but a key factor is this: low budget movies inspire me. In the current sea of carbon-copy blockbusters, they are often the most creative things going.

EQUINOX certainly fits that bill, and I'm glad that it came into my life when it did. It sure as hell changed it forever.

EQUINOX, DOWN UNDER

by John Harrison

I initially thought **EQUINOX** something of an unusual choice of film for the first roundtable discussion to appear within the pages of *Monster!* But then, *Monster!* seems to pride itself on being different from all the other genre magazines around, making the choice strangely ideal and certainly unique.

I didn't grow up with **EQUINOX**. I had read about it in several fanzines I had obtained in the late 'Seventies, but never had a chance to actually see it. It wasn't a film that showed-up on Australian television, and I never saw it around on home video during the 1980s (it *was* released over here on VHS at the time, on the infamous King of Video label, but it was hard to find a store that carried it; it certainly wasn't on the shelves at St. Kilda Video, where I worked weekends during the late 'Eighties).

My first actual glimpse at **EQUINOX** didn't come until 2004, when I finished my shift at Polyester Books and wandered down to the Cobra Bar for one of their regular Sunday night sessions of Super 8 film screenings. The Cobra Bar was an

exotic, jungle-themed cocktail bar which sat atop the grimy Tote Hotel in the Melbourne suburb of Collingwood, its bamboo walls adorned with framed posters and lobby cards from films like **COBRA WOMAN** (1944) and **CULT OF THE COBRA** (1955, both USA). Every Sunday evening, Phillipa, the blonde Jayne Mansfield-obsessed barmaid and hostess, would set up the Super 8mm projector on the bar, and the small but enthusiastic crowd of punters would snack on pizza, sip cool beers or exotic cocktails, and watch whatever assortment of digest reels, shorts and trailers had been brought along that night. There was usually a sci-fi or horror angle to the screenings—on one occasion, I brought along my 400' 3D reels of **IT CAME FROM OUTER SPACE** (1953) and **CREATURE FROM THE BLACK LAGOON** (1954, both USA) to screen, along with a bunch of homemade cardboard 3D glasses. Fun nights that are much missed, for sure!

It was at one of these Cobra Bar screenings that I saw the original **EQUINOX** theatrical trailer, which Phillipa owned. I dug the trailer, with the voiceover dramatically booming out the film's title over and over, and soon after I sourced a copy of the film itself from a trading partner, a DVD burn of a rather grainy VHS release, where it was retitled **THE BEAST**. A couple of years later, I was finally able to experience the film properly, thanks to Criterion's stunning DVD release of it.

For me, **EQUINOX** is one of those movies which epitomize the triumph of creativity and imagination over budget. While it's not a film that had any kind of deep emotional impact on me, whenever I watch it I can't help but think of that now long-gone era when low-budget genre films were still being shot on actual film rather than with a digital camera, and edited on a Moviola in an attic rather than pieced together on a free computer software program. When fans became filmmakers and tried to do something bold and unique with very little money, rather than throw together another generic zombie movie, and they didn't have ready-made promotional tools like Facebook and YouTube to get their creations out there, having to rely on publications like *Cinefantastique* and fanzines such as *Gore Creatures* to spread the word, and sweet talk promoters and exhibitors to give their films some exposure in an actual theater or drive-in. I'm waxing nostalgic here I know, but this is the kind of fertile low-budget filmmaking scene that I would have loved to have grown-up being a part of. An era that seemed to culminate and come to an end with Sam Raimi's **THE EVIL DEAD** (1981, USA)—a film which, ironically, is thought to have been influenced by **EQUINOX**.

It would certainly be unfair, however, for me to simply relegate **EQUINOX** to its time and place,

as there is so much about the film to admire nearly half a century later. Apart from its economical yet still-impressive use of stop-motion, cel animation and other special and practical effects, there's the appearances by noted genre writer Fritz Leiber, producer/distributor Jack H. Harris (**THE BLOB** [1958, USA]) and the voice of Forrest J. Ackerman to make fans of that era smile. But for me, the most endearing and impressive aspect of **EQUINOX** is just its uniquely strange and surreal ambiance, a coalescing of classic *Famous Monsters* with elements of Lovecraft, Ray Harryhausen and a sense of that late-'60s occult fascination which filled the pages of many pulp paperbacks, periodicals and Sunday newspaper supplements at the time.

A classic midnight cult film which still remains largely unknown by the masses, and one whose experimentation and wizardry seems to be sorely missing from today's low-budget filmmaking scene.

"Yes, I saw many pics from this movie in Uncle Forry's magazine, and read erroneously that it was ripped-off by **THE EVIL DEAD** as well, so when the Criterion DVD came out I was one *happy* nerd! That's when I found out the whole story about the two different cuts of the movie. So, when I finally got my grubby, sleazy, geeky hands on it I was relieved that it lived up to its promise. And which cut do I prefer? In my eyes, choosing between **EQUINOX** #1 and **EQUINOX** #2 is like choosing between a redhead or a brunette: they are both awesome in their own ways. I truly loved Jack Woods as Asmodeus; he was my kind of sleazy demonic pervert! When I saw it, this movie made my jaw drop with the amazing stop-motion work by David Allen. In short, this is a classic, and one of the movies I bring up as a point when I say I miss the good old days of stop-motion animation."

–Steven Ronquillo, esq.

THE OCCULT BARRIER BETWEEN GOOD AND EVIL!

by Stephen R. Bissette

Jim Duron as the live-action not-so-jolly green giant demonin Dennis Muren/Mark Thomas McGee/Jack Woods' **EQUINOX** (1970), which also featured stop-motion monsters animated by the late, great David Allen (1944-1999)

Since I'm just one of many *Monster!* contributors writing about **EQUINOX** (1967/70, USA) here, I'll spare you the usual backstory and historical context for the film itself, and no need to get into story points, I reckon. I'm sure someone else has already covered all that.

If we haven't, the Criterion **EQUINOX** 2-disc DVD release offers every possible scrap of background you could wish for, along with the original edit of the movie—the amateur labor-of-love feature that launched a clutch of careers—along with the Jack H. Harris theatrical version my generation saw in the drive-in or on late-night television. It's all there, in one tidy package, and I still can't believe this Criterion DVD exists.

After all, from 1969 on, **EQUINOX** was a rumor, a whisper, an image, a *dream...*

———

EQUINOX was known to most of us, at first, only as a title—evocative in and of itself—and an

image. Depending on which newsstand monster magazine or which fanzine you'd lucked into in the late 1960s or early 1970s, the image was most likely either a tantalizing photo of the winged Satanic demon or of the stop-motion ape-like tusked demon. In either case, it was a definite hook, and in subsequent months and years these were all the more alluring for how completely out-of-reach, out-of-sight the movie remained.

Famous Monsters of Filmland ran two images early on—a full-page "You Axed For It" shot of the winged demon (in *FM* #53, January 1969), and later a full-page black-and-white shot of that glorious **EQUINOX** advertising art (in *FM* #81, December 1970). The latter sported a caption citing Fritz Leiber (already a favorite author for me) as having a role—specifically as a "Lovecraftian Seeker of Forbidden Knowledge", the first overt association of H.P. Lovecraft with this film to see print—and mention that *FM* editor Forrest J. Ackerman was in the movie, too, as a voice delivering "the Tape Recorder's Message of Terror!"

As with many movies Forrest J. Ackerman would reference with a single photo and teaser caption, what was most confounding was FJA's phrasing or framing of every fleeting reference, as if this mysterious movie was somehow a known quantity to some of the readership. I mean, there was a list of names under that *FM* #53 "You Axed For It" photo—*somebody* had seen it, apparently, so it was "see-able." *But what the hell was this movie?* What was I missing? Why was there never *any* information, however vague, about what **EQUINOX** could possibly be? It was as alluring and baffling as such *Famous Monsters of Filmland* "constants" as **MUTANO THE HORRIBLE**: an exotic movie title cited, again and again; rarer still, a photo linked to the title, sans any explanation or context (see p.103).

What gradually became manifest, though, was that *this* was a monster movie made by fellow fans, for monster lovers.

—

By the time I was in high school, a wee bit more of the movie was finally in reach—it was in my own collection of 8mm monster movie reels, and frequently threaded up in my projector for another viewing.

As an avid collector of 8mm monster movies, I somehow found and screened the 50-foot short reel of **EQUINOX** first. It wasn't much, really, but it was something, and I quickly tracked down a copy of the 200-foot longer reel by mail-ordering it directly from Ken Films.

Like most 8mm and Super 8 movie "cutdowns", the reels were silent—and in black-and-white. The 50-foot reels were mere minutes in duration, the 200-foot reels almost 12 minutes long: more than a preview trailer, less than a movie.

Whoever was behind the selection and editing of these stripped-down highlight reels rarely demonstrated much passion for the presentations, though the labels themselves evidenced different levels of care in that department.

Blackhawk Films was the aristocracy of 8mm collecting: complete, incredibly rare films, mostly from the silent era, lovingly restored from whatever elements still existed. Those were available *only* via direct mail order from Blackhawk.

Those were entirely different from the rest of the 8mm and Super 8 films available. What we found in department stores in the 1960s—the first attractively packaged consumer-targeted sales of movies in public retail venues, predecessor to the video rental revolution of the 1980s—were the mass-market 8mm and Super 8 offerings from Castle Films, Ken Films, and (harder to find) Repub-

lic Pictures. There was also a label that sold a few movies with soundtrack records (!) that you would cue up to synchronize the sound and the movie; I had a few of their titles, too (**THE CURSE OF FRANKENSTEIN, HORROR OF DRACULA, COSMIC MONSTERS**, etc. [see *Monster!* #13 for coverage of those first two cited titles]).

Castle Films reels, complete with subtitles and even explanatory intertitles at times, offered the most satisfying selections, delivering more story content and more spectacle than, say, Ken Films usually did. Ken Films offered rather confounding edits, selected and patched together with little apparent rhyme or reason, often leaving out the meat of the movie being excerpted, so to speak. I learned this very early in my 8mm collecting years, with Ken Films' reel of **THE GIANT BEHEMOTH** (1959, UK; released on 8mm as early as 1961 [see *Monster!* #'s 7 and 12]), which was blissfully free of much Willis O'Brien/Pete Peterson animation footage (I recall only the clumsy shots of the dinosaur swimming underwater). The bulk of the **BEHEMOTH** reel (both 50-foot and 200-foot) comprised the risible rod-puppet "Behemoth" ferry boat sequence (see *Monster!* #12, pp.94-96).

EQUINOX was a Ken Films release.

The bulk of the excerpted footage was nonsensical, but entertaining enough—introduction of the 20-something-year-old "teenage" heroes on their picnic, glimpses of the Necronomicon-like book responsible for all the hubbub, and the giant that was an actor in makeup and shaggy caveman-like

Cover to one of the mail-order *Blackhawk Films Bulletins*, from which one could order rarities like Georges Méliès short films, F.W. Murnau's **NOSFERATU**, and much more

garb attacking our heroes, intent on recovering the book—but the climactic winged demon stop-motion animation sequence was the absolute highlight. *That* was what I ran the reel to watch again and again, despite the brevity of the stop-motion on view.

Still, Ken Films packaging was always sweet eye candy. It was the **EQUINOX** cover art that *really* grabbed me, promising action and monsters that were M.I.A. from the 8mm reel itself. This was the full-color version of the promo art shown in *FM* #81. The cartoony color graphic looked like a Matt Fox *Weird Tales* or 1950s Pre-Code comicbook cover, the title block lettering practically shouting *"Eeeeeqqqquuuiiinoxxx!"* Front and center was that wonderful Kong-like tusked ape-creature, arms raised with a victim clutched in one fist, its chest bloodily pierced by a spear—a creature frustratingly not included in the Ken Films 8mm footage—and so this further taste only whet my appetite for the Real McCoy.

EQUINOX was still a great unknown. Only a little of its mystery had been resolved, enhancing the promise of what was still unseen, unheard, and unknowable.

———

I still can't sort out how it would have been so that the Ken Films 8mm reels were sold before the movie itself played in our neck of the woods, but there ya go. That's how it happened.

My jaw fell open when I saw the newspaper ad for **EQUINOX** in *The Times Argus* (Barre, VT). It had at last arrived! There, in black and white, was a fragment of that artwork I'd studied in *Famous Monsters* and on the Ken Films cover art—the Jack Harris advertising art, as it turned out—and that title graphic:

EEEEQQQUUUUIIIINNNOOOXXXXX!!!

Lucky me, at sweet sixteen years of age I had my driver's license, so I could drive myself the fifteen or so miles from home to the Twin City Drive-In on the Barre-Montpelier Road and see it that very night, double-billed with **BEWARE! THE BLOB**

(a.k.a. **SON OF BLOB**). Jack H. Harris rolled that sequel out in 1972, so that's the year I finally saw **EQUINOX**, sometime in late June or early July.

Going it alone—none of my friends cared to go with me—I arrived early, snagging the perfect central spot for the car for the optimum windshield visibility, popping out to get sufficient popcorn and soda for the duration, then hooking up the speaker to the car window and settling in for whatever was to come.

Having grown up with the Holy Trinity of Jack Harris monster movies—**THE BLOB** (1958), **THE 4D MAN** (a.k.a. **MASTER OF TERROR**, 1959), and **DINOSAURUS!** (1960, all USA), all via TV (and in color, since we had one color TV set in our front room)—there was a look, sound, and feel to movies produced by Harris that shaped whatever expectations I harbored that night.

Both movies confounded those: this was, after all, the early 1970s, and even the Blob went with the flow. **BEWARE! THE BLOB** was weird, staccato, abrasive and at times funny, starring Godfrey Cambridge (who I'd recently seen in **WATERMELON MAN** [1970, USA]; he's devoured by the Blob in his living room chair in the opening minutes), Robert Walker, Jr. (indelibly, iconically *Star Trek*'s dangerous "Charlie X" to my generation, though he was also one of the commune hippies I'd recognized in **EASY RIDER** [1969, USA]), and even Burgess Meredith (The Penguin!) in a cameo as a wino (with director Larry Hagman, recognizable in those pre-*Dallas* days only for *I Dream of Jeanie*). The pitch-black humor of **BEWARE! THE BLOB** had almost nothing to do with the Harris movies of yore. Only the bright-red blob itself was a touchstone to the Harris/Irvin S. Yeaworth, Jr. era, and there was very little of Yeaworth's Christian conservatism on view in **BEWARE! THE BLOB**.

———

My heart raced a little as the second feature splashed across the drive-in screen. Fun as **BEWARE! THE BLOB** had been, I was here for **EQUINOX**.

I was not disappointed.

What no doubt put off most audiences about **EQUINOX** on the big screen lit candles in my heart: it *looked and felt like a student movie*, and that wasn't a bummer for me, it was a joy. I was transfixed, mesmerized. I wasn't going anywhere except where **EQUINOX** led me.

Needless to say, as a stop-motion animation junkie from childhood, I was in 7th heaven whenever the movie's effects graced the screen. The story, such as it was, did its job linking the monster set-pieces,

The pressbook cover for **EQUINOX**'s "X"-rated (!) UK theatrical release, double-billed with **BIGFOOT** (see *Monster!* #3, p.36)

which couldn't last long enough for me. The blue simian (Taurus by name, I at some point divined over a decade later when a copy of the 1970 movie fanzine *Ready for Showing* Vol. 1, No. 1 fell into my hands) was my favorite by far, succumbing

An 8 ft. giant named TAURUS (a cross between an ape and a bull dog) from "The Equinox".

COLLECTOR'S EDITION

much too quickly to that spear in the chest. Even the green fur-clad ogre from the Ken Films cutdown was more appealing in full color. These creatures were all intent upon recovering The Book from the picnicking "kids," and for their trespasses the hapless picnic quartet would pay with their souls and their lives before the film's grim coda (which wasn't much of a surprise by 1972, since George Romero's **NIGHT OF THE LIVING DEAD** and Bob Kelljan's **COUNT YORGA, VAMPIRE** had popularized the downbeat twist finale for almost all subsequent drive-in horrors).

Whatever Jack H. Harris and director/packager Jack Woods did to and with the original Dennis Muren/Mark McGee feature film (changes we now know and can identify, but at the time there was nowhere or no way to find out), **EQUINOX** matched and transcended any and all of my expectations. A couple of cars gave up and drove out of the drive-in lot during the film, giving up; well, it was getting late, but I doubt it worked for the average audience. I loved and responded to its roughhewn nature. Its very crudity—including the crass addition of the demonic "forest ranger" Mr. Asmodeus, played by Jack Woods—was intoxicating. This was a bizarre crash-course in filmmaking, *if one only had eyes to see.* And oh, I did—I did. The crazy-quilt shift of old and newer footage was readily apparent, emphasized by the ever-changing color palette. The characters changed dramatically without rhyme or reason, despite the roles being played throughout by the same quartet of lead players: their hairstyles and hair-lengths changed and they'd look younger, then older, in various shots and sequences. Was anyone else in the cars surrounding me noticing this? Would they care if they did? The whole confection was off-kilter and disorienting, but it was a lot of fun.

Still, it was hard to nail down what precisely **EQUINOX** was, or was even *like.* I'd read a lot of H.P. Lovecraft by this point in life, and it initially struck me that the Lovecraftian angle FJA had cited in *Famous Monsters* was honest enough. I dug the discovery and narrative role of the *Necronomicon*-like book responsible for all the interdimensional passages, portals, and transgressions. Then again, this *wasn't* Arkham, Massachusetts: it was southern California, already overly-familiar after a lifetime of movie and prime-time TV viewing.

In short order, the movie took a more playful path. These protagonists weren't obsessed scholars uncovering dark secrets of primordial God-like beings; they were clean-cut college students on a picnic, utterly chaste in their relationships with one another, and the creatures they accidentally conjured or encountered were movie monsters,

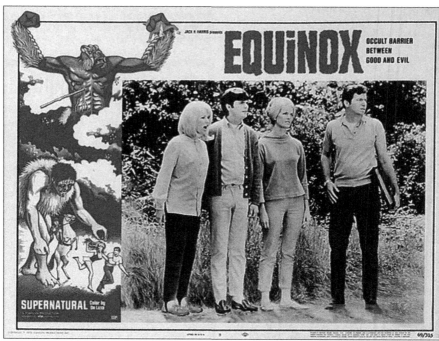

The "teenage" (!) cast of **EQUINOX** *[from left to right]*: Robin Christopher, Frank Boers, Jr. (better-known later in his career as Frank Bonner), Barbara Hewitt and Edward Connell

pure and simple. The most demonic of them all—the true form of the sneering, drooling Asmodeus—spread its bat-wings and soared from more classical mythological and Judeo-Christian iconography, recalling Doré's Biblical Fallen Angel and Harryhausen's reptilian harpies.

The permeable dimensional barrier/portal, the fairy-tale castle, odd eruptions of magic, and the frantic back-and-forth shenanigans of the put-upon heroes smacked of fantasy rather than horror, with nary a goosebump or hackle raised. It was entertaining enough and had its own flavor, but it was hardly Lovecraft. For me, only one image in the entire movie truly echoed what I loved most about Lovecraft's fiction: the all-too-fleeting glimpse of a stop-motion-animated land cephalopod attacking Fritz Leiber's country cottage in a flashback. In those precious seconds of screen time, **EQUINOX** proved budget wasn't what stood in the way of Lovecraft's stories being properly translated to the silver screen. If only **THE HAUNTED PALACE** (1963) or **THE DUNWICH HORROR** (1970, both USA) had briefly incorporated such startling imagery!

Mr. Asmodeus and the deranged old man laughing in the cave (played by Dennis Muren's grandpa) were the silliest characters. Mr. Asmodeus—with his garish makeup, park ranger's uniform, and his magic ring—was the goofiest of all, especially when he sexually assaulted one of the female leads. This attack involved hilarious, exaggerated close-up shots of Woods/Asmodeus mugging and slavering for the camera. Rape is never funny, but it was hard to do anything but laugh at such shamelessly over-the-top ham.

EQUINOX was, above all, inspiring. Mind you, I'd been experimenting with making my own 8mm and Super 8 movies for a few years by that time, primarily working with my high school pals Bill Hunter and Alan Finn. Our antics included our timid experimentation with crude stop-motion clay animation and effects, the most elaborate and time-consuming of which was staging the climactic decay of M. Valdemar for a planned adaptation of the Edgar Allan Poe tale. Alas, what took days to film, frame-by-frame, passed by in seconds once the developed film arrived and prompted high hilarity (as Valdemar's clay face—constructed by me on a Renwall human skull model—appeared to vertically unzip and flop apart).

EQUINOX unreeled like the best-ever homemade monster movie, better than the one I'd long been concocting in my own noggin. All the telltale signs of its amateur origins were evident, but this was the **GONE WITH THE WIND** of amateur monster movies. As such, it was glorious and inspiring. It made me want to tinker with making my own movies once more, and definitely fired-up the desire to write and draw my own stories and comics with more determination.

Point-Of-View Rape: Woods as Asmodeus

I went back to catch the entire double-bill again the following night. I was trying to brand every frame of **EQUINOX** into my brain, certain that I'd never see it again in my lifetime. It played one more night—a Sunday—but I couldn't justify borrowing my parent's car again to revisit movies I'd already seen twice.

Then it was gone.

Gone... *forever?*

———

Hardly.

In later years, **EQUINOX** enjoyed a most curious afterlife.

At first, it remained a harbinger in *Famous Monsters*. **EQUINOX**'s (soft) bummer finale was among the "shock endings" detailed in the solid article on twist horror movie finales and codas in *Famous Monsters of Filmland* #94 (November 1972). Around this time, **EQUINOX** was advertised as one of the 8mm and Super 8 monster movies (along with Willis H. O'Brien and Ray Harryhausen's **MIGHTY JOE YOUNG** [1949], Harryhausen's **EARTH VS. THE FLYING SAUCERS** [1956] and **20 MILLION MILES TO EARTH** [1957, all USA], and Jim

Captain Company ad from the back pages of late 1970s issues of Warren magazines, including *Famous Monster of Filmland*

From top: "Taurus", the stop-motion-animated simian demon; Asmodeus reveals his true demonic form at the climax of **EQUINOX**; Jim Hudson (Frank Bonner) uses an arcane symbol to ward off evil; Bonner as Jim's evil *doppelgänger* (actually Asmodeus in disguise)

Danforth's **WHEN DINOSAURS RULED THE EARTH** [1970, UK]) in the back pages of late issues of *Famous Monsters* and all the Warren magazines, specifically spotlit as a choice title among "Animated Monster Home Movies". However, that damned green-skinned live-action ogre was pictured in the ad (accurately enough, since that beastie dominated the Ken Films cutdown reels). Only much, much later would I learn that **EQUINOX**'s production essentially began in the pages of *Famous Monsters* in the early 1960s, reportedly via a catalytic "Graveyard Examiner" ad that brought the original teenage filmmaking team together.

Don Dohler's *Cinemagic* magazine became a staple of my reading, expanding upon the legacy of **EQUINOX** and adding a rogue's gallery of subsequent amateur SF/fantasy/horror/monster movies and filmmakers to my "must-see" list. By the time Dohler's self-published slick zine made the leap to the newsstands as a companion to *Starlog* and *Fangoria*, **EQUINOX** had become a somewhat sacred artifact, a touchstone of a new generation of filmmakers at all levels of amateurism and professionalism.

Amid all this, I did my small part to expand its do-it-yourself legacy while at Johnson State College. Though I couldn't locate a 16mm rental print of **EQUINOX** to include in the busy film programming I spearheaded from 1974-76, I *did* manage to convince JSC campus radio station manager William Price to let me script and codirect a (very) short-lived original radio TV horror anthology program entitled **EQUINOX**. Bill Price and his right-hand tech Laird worked up a dandy title spot, in which Price's Rod Serling-like introduction led into the program's title, booming over the airwaves with an echo-chambered resonance: *"The Occult Barrier Between Good and Evil: EEEEEQQQQUUIIINNNOXXXXX!!!"* Alas, the show only lasted three episodes; the first, in which excerpted phone conversations between two mothers end with one of their children being found dead—having been partially devoured by his *teddy-bear*—was considered pretty effective. Nevertheless, it bombed. For me, though, it was a hoot for as long as it lasted.

Then **STAR WARS** hit, and Dennis Muren became a name to conjure with in the science-fiction and special effects fan communities. "Hey, didn't Muren make a monster movie in his youth?"

Then *WKRP in Cincinnati* was a primetime TV hit (from 1978 to '82), and Frank Bonner a.k.a . Frank Boers, Jr. became a familiar face, enjoying celebrity far, far beyond his heroic turn in **EQUINOX**. Thereafter, whenever friends mentioned to me their having caught **EQUINOX** on late-night TV, it's Bonner/Boers' performance they chuckled over more than anything else.

When my friend Jack Venooker and I made the pilgrimage to the still-standing VT/NY state border Hathaway's Drive-In (in North Hoosick, NY, on Route 67) to catch the area premiere of **THE EVIL DEAD** (1981, USA), more than one associative link with **EQUINOX** came to mind as Sam Raimi's breakthrough "Ultimate Experience in Grueling Horror" sent folks reeling from their cars. From the discovery of the *Book of the Dead* to the subsequent unleashing of ancient demons to the critical role of an old tape-player and use of stop-motion animation (albeit for gore effects instead of Harryhausen-like creatures), I couldn't help but wonder if the **EVIL DEAD** do-or-die creative team had been inspired by **EQUINOX**. I tried to explain this to Jack, but he'd never heard of **EQUINOX**—"Only *you* see that, Bissette", I was told. Ya, well, maybe so, Jack.

Soon afterwards, as videocassettes popped up in Mom and Pop electronic shops and grocery stores throughout New England like mushrooms in cowpies after a morning rain, countless "lost" movies became accessible. This was *way* better than collecting 8mm cutdown reels! And, lo and behold, there was **EQUINOX**! I occasionally stumbled on the sun-faded box art for Charles Band's lackluster early Wizard Video release (*"Four Teenagers Fight a Devil Cult in EQUINOX"*), spending more than one afternoon revisiting the movie I'd once thought I'd never see again. The more picturesque 1985 big-box Wizard release under a new moniker, **THE BEAST**, was even more eye-catching. The big blue ape-critter on the front cover gave away the truth, and I later convinced the shop owner to sell me the tape. It holds a place of honor in my collection, still in surprisingly good shape.

When the original arcade video game *Primal Rage* hit in the 1990s, its simian monster characters (lovingly recreating the look and movement of classical cinematic stop-motion-animated creatures) sure looked like they might have been kith and kin to **EQUINOX**'s azure-blue primate-spawn demon, Taurus.

In June 2006, the unlikeliest event of all—a Criterion DVD edition of **EQUINOX**—cinched the film's stature for all time. *Finally!* Now we could experience the original movie, in its original form, as well as revisit the Harris/Woods revised theatrical version, and savor each on their own terms.

By then, **EQUINOX** was surfacing in a marketplace hip to its origins and status as the ultimate pre-**EVIL DEAD** horror "home movie". Though many expressed surprise, the Criterion treatment seemed apropos to me, given Criterion's 2001 release of Richard Gordon/Arthur Crabtree's **FIEND WITHOUT A FACE** (1958, UK). Moreover, Criterion was more attuned to marketplace

THE CALL OF CTHULHU (2005)

than anyone acknowledged, given the immediate company of DVD revelations like **MONSTER KID HOME MOVIES** (2005), **I WAS A TEENAGE MOVIEMAKER: DON GLUT'S AMATEUR MOVIES** (2006), **THE SCI-FI BOYS** (2006), and the H.P. Lovecraft Historical Society's magnificent "amateur" faux-silent-movie **THE CALL OF CTHULHU** (2005, all USA). Now we could screen a lot of amateur monster movies dating back to the early 1960s—the very movies we'd only read about or seen photos of in the pages of *Famous Monsters, Castle of Frankenstein*, and Larry Ivie's *Monsters and Heroes*—the creative continuity **EQUINOX** emerged from and belonged to wholeheartedly.

Furthermore, building on that bedrock, HPLHS/ Andrew Leman's **THE CALL OF CTHULHU** proved once and for all time that **EQUINOX**'s recipe for "homemade monster movies" was *the* correct province of truly Lovecraftian cinema, delivering the most delicious of all Lovecraft film adaptations ever. Proving lightning could strike twice, the HPLHS team upped the ante and delivered their first sound (*circa* faux-1930s cinema) Lovecraft adaptation, **THE WHISPERER IN DARKNESS** (2011, USA).

About the same time, the theatrical rollout of J.J. Abrams' **SUPER 8** (2010, USA) was plundering and providing an even richer cultural contextual companion in a much more populist arena. Set as it was in 1979—a decade after Jack H. Harris snapped up **EQUINOX** and began reshaping it into something that could play in theaters and drive-ins—**SUPER 8** more than vindicated **EQUINOX**'s standing in cinema history: it arguably sanctified it.

EQUINOX had achieved immortality, of a kind, and that's more than OK by me.

And here we be, still talking about it...

"*BLACULA*, the black avenger, rising from his tomb to fill the night with HORROR! *BLACULA*, Dracula's soul brother! Deadlier even than he! *BLACULA!* He thirsts for your blood, he hungers for your soul! Warm young bodies will feed his hunger! Hot, fresh blood will quench his awful thirst!" ...More horrifying than *DRACULA!* The black avenger: *BLACULA!*"

–Narration from AIP's US theatrical trailer

PUTTING THE BITE ON BLAXPLOITATION:

BLACULA and SCREAM BLACULA SCREAM!

by Troy Howarth

Prior to the 1970s, black actors and filmmakers were marginalized in the Hollywood system; it can be argued that they remained so for many years beyond the '70s, of course, but there's little denying that 1971 proved to be a watershed year for the black community in Hollywood. In the independent scene, Melvin Van Peebles (born 1932) unleashed **SWEET SWEETBACK'S BAADASSSSS SONG,** *which he not only directed and starred in but also produced, wrote, edited and composed its music—which was performed by the group Earth, Wind and Fire. The release of the soundtrack served to advertise the existence of the film, which was distributed independently and without the benefit of a traditional ad campaign; it proved to be a resounding success, and marked a major development in black filmmaking. That same year, a major Hollywood company—Metro Goldwyn Mayer—secured the rights to* **SHAFT.** *Directed by photographer-turned-film director Gordon Parks (1912-2006), the film presented the first truly iconic "cool" black screen hero in the form of Richard Roundtree (born 1942) as private investigator John Shaft. The combined success of these films kicked off what would be known as the Blaxploitation movement. In essence, these films allowed black actors and (occasionally) filmmakers to make films in popular genres, but with an emphasis on black characters and all that was deemed to be part and parcel of the black "experience". Some critics deride these films as perpetuating negative stereotypes, while others see them as being liberating—inevitably, some fall into the former category, while others are more representative of the latter. The Blaxploitation movement would make screen icons out of the likes of Roundtree and Pam Grier, even if the films themselves remain hotly debated to this day.*

As producers floundered about trying to figure out the next big "thing" in the horror genre, the emergence of the Blaxploitation movement must have seemed heaven-sent. Here was a fresh opportunity to gear formulaic product towards a new demographic, and it didn't even necessitate spending much in the way of money! Samuel Z. Arkoff (1918-2001) and James H. Nicholson (1916-1972), the executives at American International Pictures (AIP), were quick to seize on the notion, and a script was developed for **BLACULA.** The title was obvious enough and it had exploitation value, but it also has a level of (perhaps) unintended camp which has worked against the film being taken very seriously by many critics. More of the same would follow, however: **BLACKENSTEIN** (1973) and **DR. BLACK AND MR. HYDE** (1976) continued the trend, but nobody seemed to show any interest in "THE BLUMMY", and, sooner than go for the obvious and title their **EXORCIST** cash-in "THE BLAXORCIST", AIP went with the far-less-exploitative-sounding **ABBY** (1974). However, it is with **BLACULA** (1972) and its sequel, **SCREAM BLACULA SCREAM** (1973), that we concern ourselves, so let's turn our attention there...

Little is known about screenwriters Joan Torres and Raymond Koenig, and it seems that the extent of their credited work experience in Hollywood begins and ends with the *Blacula* films. Their script for **BLACULA** allowed AIP to cut costs by taking advantage of the burgeoning trend towards

Floridian newspaper ad for one of the tawdrier '70s Blaxploitation monster flicks

Caped To Kill: William Marshall as the batty "Blacula"—more formally known as Prince Mamuwalde—strikes a feral publicity pose as one of the most iconic of all Blaxploitation movie characters

more "mod" genre material—popularized by such films as **COUNT YORGA, VAMPIRE**, which they acquired for distribution in 1970—while also working in the requisite dose of "jive" which was designed to appeal to black audiences. AIP hired

This '70s African magazine cover seems to have been inspired by **BLACULA**

a black director, William Crain (born 1949), and aimed high with their casting for the title character. Distinguished Shakespearian actor William Marshall (1924-2003) was offered the part, and, while he knew it had the potential to lead to bigger and better things, he was also sensibly worried that the character, as written, was a stereotype of the most loathsome variety. As he would later explain, the character was originally named Andrew Brown—the name itself proving problematic, as it recalled the racially insensitive *Amos and Andy* series, which got its start on the radio in the 1920s and came to an end on TV in the 1950s. The name was deliberately intended to establish a jokey air, so Marshall believed, and the character was also written as something of a loser, a lay-about who could play into the white audiences' perceptions of blacks as indolent figures of fun. Marshall insisted upon some heavy rewriting before he was willing to sign on the dotted line, and—thank God for it—just as star Robert Quarry (1925-2009) had rescued **COUNT YORGA** from being a sex movie with some incidental horror elements, Marshall would single-handedly provide **BLACULA** with some dignity. It was Marshall who devised the idea of making the character into an African prince, named Mamuwalde, who becomes enslaved to the cult of vampirism when he gets into a racially-heated exchange with the bigoted Count Dracula. Marshall also brought in an element of pathos by bringing in a tried-and-true plot device popularized in **THE MUMMY** (1932): Mamuwalde would not just be a bloodthirsty monster, but he would also be driven by the desire to be reunited with his reincarnated love interest in the form of Tina, a modern woman who happens to be the spitting image of his late wife, Princess Luva. As he later explained in an interview with Kevin G. Shinnick, "The producers begged me to have a read of it and consider it. I hated the title. I had no love for him or them. I had a chance to read it and saw ways in which we could turn it into something more significant, working from certain periods in European and American history that had to do with the kidnapping of African people, and dragging them from their homelands. So I offered a different idea for the character, and they liked it. They gave it some thought, and they didn't seem able to come up with any ideas that were better than mine. (Laughs)"[1] With these changes, **BLACULA** became a serious horror film with a bit of pathos tossed in for good measure. Working in tandem with director Crain and a gifted supporting cast, Marshall helped to transform a distasteful piece of exploitation into one of the most purely enjoyable—and surprisingly scary—horror films of the 1970s.

The action kicks off with a prologue, in which Prince Mamuwalde (Marshall) and Princess Luva (Vonetta McGee, of Sergio Corbucci's **THE GREAT SILENCE** [*Il grande silenzio*, 1968, Italy]) are visiting Count Dracula (Charles Macaulay, of **THE HOUSE OF SEVEN CORPSES** [1974, USA]) at the latter's Transylvanian castle. The Prince and Princess are hoping to convince Dracula to sign a petition against the slave trade, but they do not realize that the Count is a raging bigot himself and sees nothing wrong with the notion of slavery. Heated words are exchanged and Dracula gets his dander up: he puts the bite on Mamuwalde and seals him in a coffin, leaving Princess Luva to rot by his side in a sealed chamber in the bowels of the castle. Centuries later, a pair of interior decorators—cue insensitive "funny" queer stereotypes; hey, we can only make so much progress in one little B movie, OK?!—negotiate to remove much of the furniture from the Castle, which has been abandoned since Dracula and his entourage were obliterated by Professor Van Helsing. Seeing the furniture and décor as the epitome of camp and kitsch, they decide to take the coffin containing Mamuwalde's slumbering body (though they do not realize this yet) back to Los Angeles with them, as well. While inventorying their Transylvanian booty, they inadvertently unleash Mamuwalde, whose thirst for blood has been exacerbated by his long-term imprisonment. Mamuwalde is then free to roam the city at large, eventually meeting a young woman named Tina

Japanese poster for the first film in the **BLACULA** duo. Thanks to Jolyon Yates, we learned that the title translates to "Bloodsucking Spirit Burakyura". A more literal alternate translation provided us by John Paul Cassidy gave it as "Vampire Blacula"

(McGee, again), whom he believes to be Princess Luva's reincarnation. Tina's sister Michelle (Denise Nicholas, of **GHOST DAD** [1990, USA]) and Michelle's boyfriend Gordon (Thalmus Rasulala, of **THE LAST HARD MEN** [1976, USA]) fear that something is not right with Mamuwalde, and Gordon becomes convinced that he has something to do with the new spate of killings which are leaving the victims drained of blood...

BLACULA does not seek to reinvent the wheel, nor does it need to do so. What is does, however, is to attack its admittedly warmed-over situations with enviable energy and relish. Director Crain is not a great stylist and much of the film is executed in a blandly efficient manner, but he pulls out all the stops where it really counts and the horror content is therefore very effective indeed. The whole thing is anchored by the sincere performances, notably by Marshall. It's easy to imagine that, in more progressive times, Marshall would have become a major film star. Born in Gary, Indiana, in 1924, he graduated from the Actors Studio and made his Broadway debut at the age of 20. In the 1950s, he served as an understudy for Boris Karloff in a Broadway production of *Peter Pan* (with Karloff playing Captain Hook, not the title character, it should be stressed!) and impressed critics with his star turn as Othello. With his imposing

---

1 Shinnick, Kevin G., "Blacula vs. Yorga: William Marshall and Robert Quarry Interviewed," *Scarlet Street* #19, 1995, p.48.

Geometric Design's **BLACULA** bust

physical presence and booming baritone voice, he had all the qualities to become a major movie star—but Hollywood wasn't quite ready for him and didn't quite know what to do with him, either. He did guest spots on such programs as *Danger Man* and *Star Trek*, but film work proved sporadic and unfulfilling. **BLACULA** provided him with his first starring role on screen, and, while it was not the most distinguished of showcases in some respects, he was not about to let the opportunity go to waste. Marshall's dedication and professionalism compelled him to insist on changes, and there's no denying that the project would have been much, much poorer without him. He is absolutely wonderful in the film, as well. He projects great humanity and intelligence as Mamuwalde, but when all bets are off and he's driven by bloodlust, he's the most terrifying bloodsucker this side of Christopher Lee's Dracula (see my overview of Hammer's series in *Monster!* #12, p.24). Indeed, Marshall's presence and line delivery cannot help but remind one of Lee's Count. The film itself may have some camp leanings, but there's nothing campy about his performance. Marshall makes the best of the occasional moments of sly humor (asking for a Bloody Mary at a night club, for example), but his performance is commendable for its sincerity; he could not have played Othello with any more commitment. Many critics have rightly pointed to Marshall as the film's saving grace, but this should not suggest that the supporting cast is

not up to par, either. Vonetta McGee (1945-2010) is an attractive and likable heroine as Princess Luva and her modern-day "reincarnation" Tina. McGee gives the character an ethereal air which makes it quite believable that she may not be quite "of this world", and she has terrific chemistry with Marshall. Thalmus Rasulala (1939-1991) is excellent as the film's *de facto* Van Helsing figure, Dr. Gordon Thomas. Thomas is brusque and condescending at times—one character memorably refers to him as "the rudest nigger I have ever seen in my life!"—but he is also quick on the uptake and proves to be a resourceful foe for Blacula. Charles Macaulay (1927-1999) gives a scene-stealing performance as Dracula—he is made up to resemble the description of the character in Bram Stoker's book, as an older man with a mustache, but he's also fitted out with a snazzy goatee and dresses every inch like a dandy. Dracula isn't just evil— he's a sneering bigot, as well, and Macaulay gets maximum mileage out of every insinuating line of dialogue he is given. It's a marvelous cameo and it really deserves to be better regarded as one of the more memorable depictions of Dracula onscreen; it's a pity he never had the chance to play the character in a vehicle of his own. Elisha Cook, Jr. (1903-1999), a veteran character actor whose credits include everything from John Huston's **THE MALTESE FALCON** (1941, USA) to Roman Polanski's **ROSEMARY'S BABY** (1968, USA), also pops up to play the ill-fated morgue attendant with the worst fake "hook for a hand" this side of a high school pantomime, but he makes a good impression anyway. And let us not overlook the wonderful Ji-Tu Kumbuka (born 1942), who plays a quirky character named Skillet; he's not in the film very much, but he's an endearing and funny presence, memorably describing Mamuwalde as "one strange dude!"

As noted above, Crain's direction is seldom very imaginative, but it gets the job done with quiet efficiency. The pacing is very good, however, and despite some rather anemic production values— which extend to some very tacky makeups for the supporting/bit part vampires—the use of real locations helps to give it a feeling of verisimilitude. The various shock scenes are extremely effective: this reviewer can still recall being utterly traumatized by some of the scenes as a child, and truth be told, I still find it genuinely scary in a few spots. There's a marvelous sequence in the morgue involving one of Blacula's victims coming back to life, for example, as well as a great attack by Blacula on the interior decorator characters who unwittingly bring him back to life—talk about gratitude! The finale of the film is also very interesting for introducing a relatively new element to the horror genre. (**SPOILER ALERT!**) The film ends with Mamuwalde sparing Dr. Thomas and committing suicide by walking out into the sunlight, driven to despair by the death of Tina. Later that same year, Spanish horror icon Paul Naschy (a.k.a. Jacinto Molina) would pick up the suicidal vampire bit and use it for the finale of Javier Aguirre's **COUNT DRACULA'S GREAT LOVE** (*El gran amor del conde Drácula*, 1973, Spain [see *Monster!* #6, p.65]). The film also gets a tremendous boost from its funky score by Gene Page (1939-1998), which includes some songs by the Hues Corporation and 21st Century Limited; the movie does rather grind to a halt to allow for some of these numbers to be performed in a couple of night club scenes, but this is a forgivable misstep given how genuinely catchy the songs prove to be.

BLACULA did not wow the critics when it was released, but it proved to be a big moneymaker for AIP—and since they were only concerned with the box office, anyway, that meant one thing: a sequel was in order! Koening and Torres was drafted back to the fold to provide another screenplay, and it also did not meet with the approval of the film's star. "I was afraid that it was going to be a very dreary story. The whole thing damned near took place solely in one house. The audience needs air. They need to get out from under a roof!"[2] Maurice Jules was brought in to pep the script up a bit, perhaps on the strength of his work

on the indie horror film **THE VELVET VAMPIRE** (1971, USA), but Marshall's fears proved to be well-founded: for all its merits, **SCREAM**

2 *Ibid*, p. 49.

A *mucho loco* Mexican lobby card for **SCREAM BLACULA SCREAM.** The stars listed hereon are actually those for **BLACULA**, not this the sequel (except for Marshall, who does reappear, of course)

THE DEVIL TOOK HER FOR HIS LOVER!

Her body is possessed,
her soul is next!

...Can any man
save her now?

Abby

...the story of a woman possessed!

R RESTRICTED

WILLIAM MARSHALL · TERRY CARTER · AUSTIN STOKER · CAROL SPEED "Abby" · JUANITA MOORE
Screenplay by G. CORNELL LAYNE · Story by WILLIAM GIRDLER & G. CORNELL LAYNE · Music Composed and Conducted by ROBERT O. RAGLAND
Produced by WILLIAM GIRDLER, MIKE HENRY & GORDON C. LAYNE · Directed by WILLIAM GIRDLER · COLOR BY MOVIELAB · ⬛
A WILLIAM GIRDLER PRODUCTION · AN AMERICAN INTERNATIONAL RELEASE

BLACULA SCREAM simply did not connect with audiences as strongly as the original had done when it came out in 1973.

In brief, the story is this: Willis (Richard Lawson, of **SUGAR HILL** [a.k.a. **THE ZOMBIES OF SUGAR HILL**, 1974, USA]), bitter over having been passed over to be the new head of a voodoo sect, decides to exact revenge. He purchases the ashes of Blacula from a witch doctor, believing that they will give him special powers. After performing a ceremony, Blacula re-rises from the grave—and promptly puts the bite on Willis. Still driven by a thirst for revenge, Willis tries to assert himself as the boss, but Mamuwalde soon puts him in his place. When Willis reveals that Lisa (Pam Grier, of Jack Hill's **THE BIG BIRD CAGE** [1972, Philippines/USA]), a member of the sect, has exceptional powers, he decides to turn to her in the hopes of finding a cure which will free him from Dracula's curse. Mamuwalde manages to charm Lisa, but she senses that there is something evil in him. Meanwhile, the death toll rises and Mamuwalde must use force to try and compel Lisa into performing an exorcism that will finally put his soul to rest...

To direct the first sequel to their founding moneymaker, AIP elected to go a different route: white director Bob Kelljan (1930-1982) was hired, based on the strength of his two popular vampire movies—the aforementioned **COUNT YORGA, VAMPIRE** and its sequel, **THE RETURN OF COUNT YORGA** (1971, USA). Kelljan brought his bag of tricks with him, and the result is frequently scary and considerably more atmospheric than the first film—but Mar-

shall's point about the claustrophobic nature of the material is well taken. Too much of the film is devoted to people wandering around looking for other characters, a problem which also plagued Kelljan's second *Yorga* feature. The impression is of trying to pad-out the running time, which is a great pity since so little is made of the potentially thrilling pairing of Marshall and Pam Grier. Even so, the film offers up some great shocks of its own, and despite its uneven pacing, it proves to be a respectable follow-up.

In addition to Kelljan's sporadically stylish direction and inventive staging, the film also benefits from moodier cinematography, which keeps things appropriately shadowy and mysterious. There is a terrific set-piece involving two of Willis' friends coming to the house, looking for him, not realizing that he and Blacula are playing cat-and-mouse with them. The bit used so effectively in the *Yorga* films with the Count approaching the camera with arms outstretched, in slow-motion, is put to good use in this sequence, too. Without a doubt, however, the film's most incendiary and memorable sequence involves Mamuwalde's showdown with a pair of black pimps. The scene is not devoid of humor, but it is basically played straight and allows Mamuwalde to vent frustration with the way in which these tacky stereotypes are exploiting their own people in order to get by. When quizzed about whether the scene was his idea or that of the filmmakers, he replied, "How could it have been theirs? That was not on their minds. They're not suffering from it. It's not often a player has very much power, but I kept insisting."[3] Unfortunately, such sequences are the exception rather than the rule and Mamuwalde's musings on the state of African-American life in the 20th Century is kept to a minimum. With a better script and a little less padding, Kelljan and company may well have ended up outdoing the original; as it stands, however, it doesn't quite recapture the freshness and vitality of Crain's initial effort.

Once again, the bulk of the film is carried on Marshall's shoulders—and once again he proves to be up to the task at hand. He may have had misgivings with the way the project was developed, but these do not manifest on screen: he's every bit as effective here as he was in the first film, though it has to be said that the feral makeup used for when he transforms into the blood-crazed Blacula is not as effective this time around. Marshall's innate intelligence and charisma help to make the character charming and intimidating, and he easily steals the film from his costars. Pam Grier (born 1949) does a good job as Lisa, but the character is not as well-de-

3 *Ibid*, p. 50.

veloped as one would have liked; one can easily imagine Grier, in full-blown **COFFY** (1973) or **FOXY BROWN** (1974, both USA) mode, holding her own against Marshall's dignified bloodsucker, but here she is required to function as a more conventional damsel-in-distress. Richard Lawson (born 1947) is a hoot as the power-mad Willis, and he gets the film's funniest moment: when the narcissistic character realizes that he can no longer see himself in the mirror, he flips out before asking Mamuwalde to let him know how he looks. Don Mitchell (1943-2013), best remembered for his recurring role of Mark Sanger on the popular '70s Raymond Burr TV series *Ironside*, is on hand to play Lisa's detective boyfriend; he does the best he can with the usual boring heroic role and makes the character much more likable and sympathetic than he might otherwise have been.

SCREAM BLACULA SCREAM failed to replicate the box office takings of the original, putting AIP off the idea of making a third instalment. Rumors have long circulated that the idea was to pit Blacula against Count Yorga, but Marshall would later claim that another AIP icon was actually on the agenda instead. "It wasn't Robert Quarry that they wanted to pit me against. It was Vincent Price. That was how Sam Arkoff saw it." The mind reels at the idea of a potential Blacula mashup with Dr. Phibes, but the film would have allowed the two series to reach their third instalment; disappointing returns ensured that both franchises stopped short at just one sequel apiece, however. Arkoff would continue to mine the potential of Marshall as the first black horror icon by casting him as the exorcist in **ABBY**, but the film proved to be a disappointment for everybody involved—and its subsequent impounding by Warner Bros. has kept the film off the market and somewhat tricky (though by no means impossible) for fans of Marshall to track down. After that, Marshall bid adieu to AIP and the horror genre, though he remained much in demand as a character actor in more "mainstream" assignments (he is among the all-star cast of Robert Aldrich's **TWILIGHT'S LAST GLEAMING** [1977, USA], for example) and continued to impress onstage as well. He would go on to become "The King of Cartoons" for a new generation of fans with his appearances on Paul Reubens' cult TV series *Pee-wee's Playhouse* from 1987 to 1990, but good roles proved to be difficult to come by. Marshall's final years were marked by the onset of diabetes and Alzheimer's disease; he finally succumbed to his ailments in 2003 at the age of 78. That he never became a bigger star is nothing short of shameful: it was never an issue of talent, but rather of narrow-minded casting directors and producers who first couldn't see past the color barrier, and then had a hard time utilizing his con-

siderable talents after perceiving him as the star of "campy" 1970s horror films. For fans in the know, however, **BLACULA** and **SCREAM BLACULA SCREAM** are emblematic of a special period in genre filmmaking—and the considerable weight, dignity and authority Marshall brought to these films is absolutely essential to their lasting appeal.

41

SHOCKING HORROR! QUICK, TURN TO PAGE 9!!!

THE RETURN OF THE REVENGE OF THE SON OF THE CURSE OF THE TOMB OF CANUXPLOITATION CRITTER CRUD CORNER!!

by Steve Fenton

One of MUFX / Emersen Ziffle's gnarly bogman/mummy-like zombie ghouls from **13 EERIE**

Much the same way as they are now, as well as back in the '80s and '90s on TV here in my adopted homeland Canada, certain inherent laws governing on-air programming (etc.) content were stringently enforced by the Canuck government, and largely still are, to some extent. Which meant/means that for every Hollywood or other foreign-made movie (or TV show, song, etc.) broadcast or screened theatrically within Canada's borders, a certain minimum percentage of produced-on-our-own-soil Canadian content—more informally and more than a little condescendingly known for decades now as "Can-con"—had/has to be shown to hopefully help counteract and compensate for the constant influx of competing foreign fare and thus keep our country's confidence in and economic support of its own national product strong; even if, while Canada produces oodles of high-quality television programming, politically correct "art-house" cinema, and the world-famous National Film Board (NFB) has long been producing all sorts of fine filmic fare, when it comes to viable exploitation flicks, we Canucks often come up sorely wanting. I mean, when **CANNIBAL GIRLS** (1973), **BIG MEAT EATER** (1982) and **HOBO WITH A SHOTGUN** (2011)—all of

which were at least partially funded by the Canadian taxpayer's hard-earned dough, whether we liked it or not—are about the best we can come up with, you know we must really be hurtin' (not that both those first two titles don't have lots to love about 'em, mind you; as for that horrendously rancid final "faux grindhouse" title though, the less said about it the better: it's a national embarrassment…at least to me, and I'm not even a citizen after being here nearly 40 years!).

Back around when I first started writing for *Monster!* in its original Xeroxed A4 newsletter incarnation, disposable Canadian-made junk like Quebecker Christian Duguay's pair of opportunistic and unnecessary "sequels" **SCANNERS II: THE NEW ORDER** and **SCANNERS III: THE TAKEOVER** (both 1991), plus Britisher Harry Bromley Davenport's **XTRO II: THE SECOND ENCOUNTER** (1990)—a belated and virtually unrelated "sequel" to the same director's much more interesting and original **XTRO** (1983, UK)—were all over the airwaves up here north of the US border. More than two decades on, little has changed on the home front in that regard, and still we Canucks are inundated with low invest-

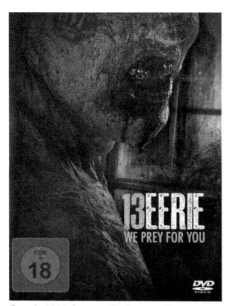

Sony's 2013 German DVD cover. This release is in English, with a native soft-subs option

io to Vancouver, British Columbia and back, anyway. And yes, I did spend about three days stuck outside Regina, Saskatchewan along the way, sheltering inside the back of an empty U-Haul trailer in the parking lot of an isolated truck-stop during what was then the worst sandstorm to hit the province in about a century. *Sigh.* Those were the days! But I digress, so I'll refrain from telling you about jumping freight trains in Brandon, Manitoba and get back on track…]).

First up is Lowell "**WOLFCOP**" Dean's low-to-no-budget zombie splatterfest **13 EERIE** (2013), which, despite all its blatantly—indeed, at times even *slavishly*—derivative/emulative "influences" and outright cribs somehow succeeded in entertaining me, albeit only at the most minimal, marginal (dare I say *gut*) level. But unlike innumerable other generic zombouts—which by now must literally be numbered in the hundreds, if not *thousands* (or so it seems)—this one has a certain indefinable "something" about it which somewhat distinguishes it from the rest of the ragtag shambling horde, and there are at least a few elements worth recommending about it, so don't be too quick to dismiss it out-of-hand as beneath you. As director Dean well-proved with his wild, witty and just plain *coolass-as-fuck* mickey-take on the lycanthropy genre, the aforementioned **WOLF-COP**, he is a highly creative filmmaker, and **13 EERIE** is very well put together for what it is and what it was made for (i.e., little more than a song).

Starting out quite strongly, the narrative is founded on a surprisingly inventive and interesting premise: a group of young hopefuls in the highly competitive, psychologically stressful and intellectually demanding field of forensic science convene at an out-of-the-way spot in the thick of the boonies—while shot in Moose Jaw, Sask., it might well be just about anywhere in the world, let alone someplace in North America—in order to undergo in-the-field research exams to determine whether they have what it takes to make it in their chosen profession. To this end, a number of evidently voluntarily donated, authentic human cadavers—by that I mean authentic within the context of the scenario, not *actual* dead bodies, natch!—have been distributed at various points around the grounds of the gone-to-seed rural facility, and it is the students' assignment to determine cause of death (etc.) for each cadaver within a designated time limit and under strict guidelines. As played with some charisma by Vancouverite Michael Shanks (likely best-known to many—if not to me—as Dr. Daniel Jackson on numerous series/episodes in the *Stargate* TV franchise), **13 EERIE**'s male protagonist Tomkins is the suitably domineering and no-bullshit character who presides over the examinations

ment/low return Canadian productions intended to help domestic broadcasters meet Can-con requirements and do their little bit to ensure our humble homegrown product isn't swamped out of existence by the competition, which, in many cases is, quite frankly, far superior (especially when it comes to trashier prefab "cult" cinema fare; case in point Jesse Thomas Cook's mostly limp **MONSTER BRAWL** [2011], that doesn't even come *close* to living up to our understandably high expectations of its killer title, which is all come-on and no payoff). Why, we've got us a thriving cottage industry of such cost-conscious "tax shelter" productions constantly going on up here! Nobody ever really expects them to be much cop, but just so long as they recoup their initial outlay and possibly even turn a bit of a profit in the process, everyone's happy as a moose in maple syrup.

Now, in terms of style and content, the following two films under review are literally poles apart. Indeed, about their only point of commonality is the fact that both were shot in, of all places, in Saskatchewan, one of western Canada's prairie provinces (which have often been used as shooting locations for incoming foreign productions—including Hollywood westerns, and even at least one Hong Kong western—due to certain basic similarities in their terrain to the American West; and make no mistake about it, all you long, tall Texans, Canada is fucking *HUGE* too! Trust me, I've hitchhiked across it, so I know [well, from Elliot Lake, Ontar-

44

with an iron hand *sans* any velvet glove and few people skills other than knowing how to browbeat into submission and bark orders at them. Initially set up to potentially be the heavy of the piece with his prickishly humorless characterization of a by-the-book, bend-no-rule authoritarian dickhead, by the end of the film he unexpectedly develops into its virtual main hero... still without being particularly likeable of a character, other than for his basic won't-back-down tenacity and stickwithitness under duress. For all his balls though, he's essentially a micromanaging, power-tripping control freak who simply can't stand the thought of *anybody*, be they living or dead, usurping his authority! But one supposes that's as good a reason as any to kick the shit out of a bunch of zombies.

Early on we see some highly convincing corpses in varying states of decomposition, and this queasiness we feel leads us to expect that things may well take a turn for the much nastier before the movie runs its course... which they intermittently do, making for some quite queasy moments of extreme horror (you'll know 'em when you see 'em! At times you can almost *smell* the oozing nastiness, slimy offal and stench of putrefaction!). Just when I was thinking this might be something a little bit (possibly even a *lot*) different, some fifteen or twenty minutes in, it dawned on me that (*yep!*) what we had on our hands here was yet another in a long line of—don't all groan at once—zombie movies; and, other than for the aforementioned forensics research angle, there is barely another single original idea in its dead head to be had here. However, for all its triteness and ultimately easily forgettable qualities, it somewhat succeeds in accomplishing what it set out to do: i.e., deliver a formulaic horror actioner brimful of cheap shocks and some good old-fashioned *SPLAT!* when needed... and those sickly-grey, snake-like intestines the zombies yank outta certain of their victims—namely the overripe already dead ones—sure did look disgustingly all-too-convincing to me. They make an unsavory and wholly unappetizing change from all the ketchup-smothered strings of raw sausages we've seen getting yanked through rupturing rubber stomach walls by Italian zombie gut-munchers and other Romero-influenced deadheads over the years. Looks-wise, those here rather resemble a cross between '80s Italo zombies and bandageless if wrinkly-skinned mummies (rather reminiscent of "bog men"), only are far more robust and lively than is the norm for either of those other two standard monster types. These things chew not just on the still-warm red-raw guts of the living or freshly deceased, but even those of long-cold and badly decomposed stiffs too; which adds an extra queasily disgusting ghoulish aspect to their foul appetite. As mentioned above, some very slippery/slimy viscera—amounting to truly awful offal indeed—add to the stomach-churning realism of the rip 'n' chomp 'n' chow-down scenes.

Due to the fact that the ambulatory corpses of prison inmates here were reanimated via toxic chemicals, the plot of **13 EERIE** seems to owe at least a bit of a debt for a good part of its base premise to John Hayes' zombie convict schlockemup **GARDEN OF THE DEAD** (1972, USA), but all similarities pretty much end there. Other than for being intended to have a built-in cultish, trendily "catchy" ring to it, the present film's title doesn't really have much more than the most superficial bearing on the movie itself, but is somewhat facilely justified by appearing onscreen as part of an unlikely address ("13 Eerie Strait Penitentiary") marked on the side of the bus which conveys the students to the research facility. The same bus later plays a major role in what amounts to the movie's action "highpoint"; and if nothing else it ought to definitely wake up any viewer who might have nodded-off in the interim.

As our sexy heroine Megan, BC-born actress Katharine Isabelle (best-known by modern monster buffs for co-starring as the title character of John Fawcett's offbeat werewolf-chick flick **GINGER SNAPS** [2000, Canada]) plays out all the typical "nice-girl-forced-to-turn-into-a-brutal-killing-machine-in-the-interests-of-personal-survival" tropes; although you kinda gotta wonder about what sort of personality type it takes for someone to wanna spend their life going elbows-deep in dead bodies... but somebody's gotta

As it proudly stated on British ads, "From the producer of **SILENT HILL + RESIDENT EVIL IV**"; so if that impresses you in any way—it sure as hell didn't impress me any!—by all means get in line. For its Spanish-subbed Hispanic DVD release, **13 EERIE** was retitled *Experimento biologico* (hmmm, whatever might *that* mean, I wonder?) and came with completely misleading cover art that tried to pass the film off as still another entry in the never-ending "zombie apocalypse" subgenre, which has pretty much been dead on its feet for at least half a coon's age now, yet still they keep on coming. Pretty well every image depicted on the front of said Hispanic vid-box doesn't appear in the actual film (howzat for misleading advertising, exploitation style?! Why, you almost have to admire its audacious arrogance).

When all is said and done, **13 EERIE**'s somewhat involving plotline along with several inventively gruesome and well-executed splatter sequences— you'll know 'em when you see 'em!—allow us to overlook all its heavy derivativeness. Just don't expect to remember too much about it a month or two after you watch it. After seeing it about six weeks ago (as of this writing), it's already fast becoming a distant memory. But you takes what you can get.

do it, I suppose, so better them than me. And the fact that Isabelle's character would even choose such an unsavory profession for herself in the first place somewhat makes her fearless, revert-to-her-killer-instincts tenacity seem more credible than if she had been some passive clerical worker or coffee shop barista who on a dime suddenly goes all macho Sigourney Weaver/Linda Hamilton on the zombies' rotten asses.

As for Armen Evrensel's utterly non-analogous and nonsensical "sci-fi parody" (such a facile label, that!) **SPACE MILKSHAKE** (2012)—which I'm quite frankly utterly amazed has racked-up an undeservedly whopping 6.0 rating at the IMDb!— it's another beast entirely, pun intended. A "WTF were they thinking?!" movie if ever there was one, its unabashedly and seemingly intentionally witless script was evidently written out in block caps with a chisel-tip Sharpie® on the back of a 2"x 2" Post-It® note. It is so resolutely moronic in fact that you almost (*almost!*) find yourself admiring the writers' audacity in slapping together such trivial tripe; this quite possibly done over a single six-pack of beers on a mini-bender one slow Friday or Saturday night; that's how slapdash and hurried it all appears. But, strange as it may seem, despite its utterly meaningless title and many other meaningless—arguably even *pointless*—things in it besides, **SPACE MILKSHAKE** somehow manages to be enjoyable, if accepted strictly on its own retardo terms...so be prepared to dumb yourself down some (assuming you're not dumb enough already, that is! ☺ [But if you're reading *Monster!* how could you be? ☺ ☺]).

Having wangled himself a far-from-cushy entry-level position on the Sanitation Station Regina—a glorified garbage scow (named, perhaps

disrespectfully, after Saskatchewan's capital!), whose sole function is to collect and dispose of drifting refuse wherever they find it—Jimmy (played by Toronto native Robin Dunne) becomes the doormat and gopher for his mostly unfriendly crewmates. Amounting to a real cinch for the casting director, this "skeleton crew" numbers a mere three other persons: Valentina (Amanda Tapping), Tilda (Kristin Kreuk), and their bossy blowhard skipper, Captain Anton Balvenie (played by Scotsman Billy Boyd, who somehow makes his supremely obnoxious character likeable—go figure!—and puts in the most manically over-the-top performance seen herein).

Earth disappears in the blink of an eye, leaving just the Regina floating in empty space where our planet used to be. It develops that the proletarian crew's isolated space station is the nexus point of all the universe's damaged realities (or words to that effect), and that a demented displaced Earthling scientist trapped in the twelfth dimension needs to get his hands on a missing Time Cube in order to restore order to the universe and the Earth back to its orbit (yadda-yadda-yadda). Going into other plot "details"—many of which seem to have been made up at random on the fly without much in the way of thought being put into them, as though they really didn't think it mattered much, so why bother—would be the height of futility. Suffice to say that a *rubber ducky* plays a major catalytic role in the story: whether he likes it or not (he *doesn't*), this is what Prof. Pinback has involuntarily been morphed into over in the 12-D, and he is understandably anxious to resume his normal human form ASAP, if at all doable (which it *ain't*, as it happens). Although the actor's actual human face is never seen onscreen, ex-*Star Trek*'s Mr. Sulu and current online mega-celeb George Takei voices the duck in his familiarly hammy manner; and we can only wonder whether the "big name" guest star ever actually met any of his "costars" eye to eye in the flesh, or whether he simply phoned his lines in via Skype, cash in advance, no questions asked. At first all the duck does is blink its cartoony googly eyes into the camera so as to "subtly" let us know that within it there resides a sentient entity, which wants out, and gets its wish. The duck's ass shortly sprouts stringy tentacles and it proceeds to go for a swim in the tub while Valentina is taking a bubble bath...the howler punch-line of this brilliant sight-gag is that she doesn't notice a thing because of all the soapsuds, and harmlessly squishes the floundering ductopus without realizing it. Shot in CG shadow-shape, the partially transformed duck subsequently mutates into something bigger and badder, if not much less ridiculous-looking than it was in its original form (i.e., that of the standard kiddies' bath toy molded in yellow plastic,

After directing **13 EERIE** in 2013, Lowell Dean went on to direct the far more consistently memorable and overall more original **WOLFCOP** (2014), which amounts to one of the coolest Canuxploitation critter flicks in recent memory

complete with benignly smiling bill). For the next "phase" of its development, the creature becomes a patently phony foam rubber octopoidal thing, non-fatally attacks assholish space skipper Anton with all the animation of an oversized, under-stuffed Beanie Baby, then slithers off into the bowels of the ship, presumably via its air ducts, as per the usual trope. The self-consciously goofball special makeup and practical creature FX were handled by Emersen Ziffle, whose recent work also includes the aforementioned Lowell Dean's amazingly entertaining **WOLFCOP** (2014, Canada [see *Monster!* #8]).

English-born, Canadian-based actress Tapping is a veteran of such American/Canadian co-production SF teleseries as *The X Files* (1993-2002) and the reboot version of *The Outer Limits* (1995-2002); appearing in a single episode of each of those two cult hits. She is best-known for starring as Major Samantha Carter on the long-running show *Stargate SG-1* (1997-2007), and she recently voiced a CG version of the same character in a spinoff video game. She also played a recurrent character on the short-lived horror series *Supernatural* (2012-2013, USA). So, all that said, how in Hades hell she ever found her way into this spaced oddity is anybody's guess. I'd imagine there may well be some "in-jokes" to her Carter character from *SG* herein, but since I have never watched a single entire episode of any of the shows in that franchise and shan't be getting around to doing so anytime soon, I wouldn't have a clue if there are or not.

As for **SPACE MILKSHAKE**, it's all so retardedly remedial that you can't help but find it endearing…to a *point*. Halfhearted elements of the amazing *Red Dwarf* TV series and Stuart Gordon's **SPACE TRUCKERS** (1996, USA) plus even a bit of that amiable if forgotten '80s **ALIEN** send-up **THE CREATURE WASN'T NICE** (a.k.a. **SPACESHIP** or **NAKED SPACE**, 1981, USA) are also thrown into the blender/mulcher, and some of the ingredients mix "well" (note quotes), while others…er, *not-so*. For instance, one of the characters ("Pinback") is tokenly named after Dan O'Bannon's character in John Carpenter's cult spaced-out SF spoof **DARK STAR** (1974, USA), as though merely dropping that famous name somehow places the present film in the same stellar company as the Carpenter one simply by association. Which is by no means to say that **SPACE MILKSHAKE** is a total write-off (other than of the tax variety, that is). It's the commitment and likeability of the talented if tiny cast which makes it "work" (note quotes); though it's hard to imagine this being anywhere even close to so endurable/enjoyable if it was played by lesser actors. About the least interesting is Dunne's blandly overeager hero; one of whose main character traits seems to be bland over-eagerness, so I suppose you could say that Dunne captures the character he was cast to play fairly well. And when it comes to material this dense, it definitely takes a certain kind of player to pull it off with any deal of conviction, which the film's cast for the most part manage to do.

To wrap-up, both the above-discussed movies are worth at least a single viewing, but it is more than likely **SPACE MILKSHAKE** which might most try viewers' patience; you're either into this sort of foolishness and "get it", or you're not, and don't. Of the pair, it would probably have a tougher time finding its "core" audience. As for **13 EERIE**, I've actually re-watched it a second time since my initial viewing, and I decided I do kind of like it quite a bit. I really don't think I'll be giving it a third spin anytime soon though (if ever), not because I don't consider it worthwhile but simply because there are so many other things still left to see, and, now that I'm (gulp) *fifty-fucking-five*, I really don't have the time to re-watch minor movies over and over again. Indeed, there are even old favorites I rarely revisit much anymore (they tend to pile up over the decades), so it rather goes without saying that I shan't be coming back for seconds of **SPACE MILKSHAKE**. It was fun enough to see once, but sometimes once is more than enough.

TERRORVISION

Reviewed by Eric Messina

USA, 1985. D: Ted Nicolaou

Narration from Empire's US trailer: *"The Putter-mans are just a typical American family. The only thing they're missing is a pet. But have we got a surprise for them. You see, Stanley Putterman's new satellite TV has just gone on the blink, and it's drawn in a creature from outer space. Like all new pets, this one's causing a little trouble around the house, and he's eating the Puttermans out of house and home [BURP!!!]. In fact, it seems like this creature will eat* anything*! Well, just about anything... Now, it's up to the kids to break the creature of its bad habits, but he's not responding well to discipline... The Puttermans finally got themselves a pet—but they never even had a chance to give it a name!"*

For years, this Charles Band production was only available on VHS and it took me forever to see this flick, mainly because I detest most of the Band clan's catalog (Albert and Richard respectively). Films with the Band brand have always been a struggle for me to endure (and this is pre-*Puppet Master* franchise / **EVIL BONG** junk, before the shit really hit the fan)! I count this film along with David Schmoeller's **TOURIST TRAP** (1978, USA), as well as both Stuart Gordon's **FROM BEYOND** (1986, USA) and **DOLLS** (1987, USA) as among the best films attached to the wretched catalog of mostly unwatchable dreck that this company has consistently churned out over the years.

Futuristic trash like **METALSTORM: THE DE-STRUCTION OF JARED-SYN** (1983, USA)— which I saw in classic red and blue Anaglyph 3D with my dad when I was 7 at a movie theater in NYC—and **PARASITE** (1982, USA) made me

leery about even bothering watching **TERROR-VISION**. But I knew I'd eventually get around to it, because the video box cover was super cool and that slobbering monster really drew me in. I'm almost embarrassed to say that the first time I got to see it was via Netflix streaming. This film is a time capsule of bad '80s fashions that attempts to show the repercussions of intergalactic hazardous waste. Cold War science fiction paranoia flicks like William Cameron Menzies' **INVADERS FROM MARS** and Roy Rowland's bizarre—if not typically Cold War-era—**THE 5,000 FINGERS OF DR. T** (both 1953, USA) were two examples that influenced director Ted Nicolaou when he devised the concept for this film.

On the garbage planet of Pluthon, two green alien sanitation workers are in the middle of flushing a revolting slimy pile of corrosive monster waste, which we later find out is really just a giant space dog that they no longer want to deal with. But *where* does the intergalactic refuse go once it's been disposed of...? That concept triggers the premise of this film. The opening shots remind me of Fred Dekker's high-grade monster trash epic **NIGHT OF THE CREEPS** (made the following year): there's a similar evil alien race that unleashes germ warfare onto planet Earth. The difference in this film however is that Pluthar, the alien garbage man played by William Paulson, feels responsible enough to send out a broadcast which constantly warns the Earth citizens—I mean, at least he's sorry for dropping a slobbering great plague into their laps! John Carl Buechler's effects really shine, and look spectacular in this one (the lead beastie would make a perfect '80s *Fangoria* cover or at least a Scream Greats poster).

Most of the cast here are some of my most favorite cult actors, starting with the sultry Mary Woronov, plus Gerrit Graham and Diane Franklin (one actress I've always had a major crush on, ever since I saw her in Damiano Damiani's **AMITYVILLE II: THE POSSESSION** [1982, USA/Italy/Mexico], which is just *disturbing*, when I think about it; maybe I should've said Savage Steve Holland's **BETTER OFF DEAD** [1985, USA], but I'd rather just tell the truth instead).

I like the ultra-high tech '80s gadgets featured in the present movie—which I'm sure are all now in a landfill somewhere—and the *über*-sexual Patrick Nagel-style décor that instantly dates the film in the fondest way possible. The production designer was Giovanni Natalucci, who worked on John Carl Buechler's **TROLL** and David Schmoeller's **CRAWLSPACE** (both 1986, USA/Italy), and also briefly for Lucio Fulci (*circa* 1974-75). In fact, this entire movie looks like a coked-out Day-Glo fever dream! I've read other reviews that try to pretend it's some kind of underlining statement about the "Me Generation", but all of that seems implied here; if anything, it's all so contrived and cartoony that it's difficult for me to find any kind of social statement against such things as the '80s nuclear family or Reaganomics herein. The film actually kind of celebrates the stupidity of that time period, but **TERRORVISION** definitely does lampoon the MTV generation (which, looking back on the current disposable Internet generation, I now consider the "good old days").

Googly-eyed suburbanite and neckerchief aficionado Stanley (Graham) Putterman and his middle class family are having major problems

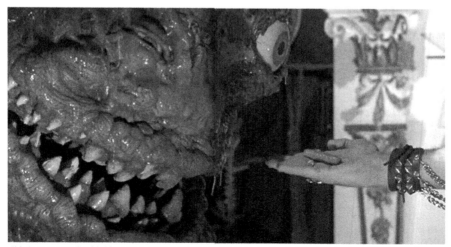

"He's a gross-lookin' booger, ain't he?! I'd nuke that sucker!" Mechanical and Makeup Imageries, Inc.'s ever-hungry TV monster eyeballs another potential snack to gobble on. It later "bites the hand that feeds" (so to speak) by chewing the guy's face off

Gorgeous Gorgon: Jennifer Richards as the cleavage-heavy horror hostess "Medusa" in **TERRORVISION**. Her late-night airing of **THE GIANT CLAW** *[inset]* is interrupted by a monstrous alien invader that emerges into our world through a TV screen

with their satellite; that is until a phantom signal bounces down from outer space just at the right time. The nasty-looking (in a good way) horror hostess Medusa—an overly sexualized version of Elvira, played by Jennifer Richards—beams onto the TV as the Puttermans settle in for some low-brow family entertainment. I like how the grandpa character says, "Monster movies are educational"! *Damn right!* I also love that wacky new wave title song by The Fibonaccis, which really kicks off the overblown, demented tone of the film in fine style.

As a suburbanite growing up in the '80s myself, I felt that none of the kitschiness was manufactured, and in my estimation...*dead right!* The war-mongering grandpa (Bert Remsen) and his grandson (Chad Allen) watch alligators dressed as dinosaurs on TV as they eat survivalist lizard beef jerky. The broken cable station that shows green solarized images reminded me of being at that adolescent age when you could flip back and forth on the squiggled scrambled *Playboy* channel in order to hopefully "accidentally" see some female flesh (or whatever your imagination would fill in the blank as). **TV**'s satellite trash monster is one of my all-time favorite Buechler creatures along with the **CELLAR DWELLAR** (1988, USA [see *Monster!* #12]). It's just incredibly gruesome!

Norton the satellite repairman, who constantly craves Heineken beers (by saying "Hey, can I grab a Heinie for the road?") is played by Sonny Carl Davis, the irate customer who causes Brad to lose his job in Amy Heckerling's **FAST TIMES AT RIDGEMONT HIGH** (1982, USA). The Puttermans are sleazy swingers who show up with another couple who are down for some boning. Their living room, which they refer to as

"The Pleasure Dome", looks like a pornographic episode of *Pee-Wee's Playhouse* on acid. Spiro the homosexual Greek swinger (played by Alejandro Rey, former costar of *The Flying Nun*!) cracks me up when he talks about how he likes "manly men" and attempts to make an ouzo margarita. He wants to have sex with Stanley, so I'm sure he'd totally be down if Gerrit Graham all of a sudden morphed into his macho "Beef" character from De Palma's **PHANTOM OF THE PARADISE** (1974, USA). After the creature devours all the swingers, they come back as mutants covered in K-Y Jelly, and the scene where they're supposed to be having an orgy for some reason reminded me of the elderly folks from **WILLY WONKA** in that they were all confined to the same bed. Suzy and her brain-dead metalhead boyfriend O.D. (played by Jonathan "Jon" Gries of **JOYSTICKS** [1983, USA] and **NAPOLEON DYNAMITE** [2004, USA] fame) constantly gawk at the camera. When O.D. gets his face chewed off as green pus squirts all over, I was glad to see him go! The monster (who grows larger by the minute) frantically flaps its jaws and resembles a skinless puppy covered in gelatinous pink scar tissue or Jabba the Hutt with one lazy eye and a zonked-out ocular whopper. The MTV generation attempts to teach the alien about health food, junk food and—most important of all—*heavy metal!*

Guttural stomach-like noises and a bulging eyeball, belonging to the alien, consistently pour from the TV set, and this seems like some sort of nod to Quentin Lawrence's **THE TROLLENBERG TERROR** (a.k.a. **THE CRAWLING EYE** (1958, UK [see *Monster!* #12]). The monster has the ability to control the grandpa once he's been devoured. After regurgitating his severed head down in the bomb shelter, it starts talking, claiming that everything is fine. When Pluthar the Martian garbage man shows up on cable, warning people to destroy their satellites for 200 Earth years, they think it's just some wacky foreign station. Busty Medusa seems hard-up to get to any party, even ones that her viewers invite her to. She royally screws everything up by suffocating Pluthar, who appears on Earth. I felt bad for him, as his face disintegrates into a viscous smear. Didn't she learn anything from sitting through all those B-movies; like that you shouldn't kill the good alien?!

Sherman (Chad Allen) has an arsenal of weapons he inherited from his grandfather, and they come in handy throughout most of the alien invasion. If we try to put a social statement on the film, it feeds into the war-mongering attitude of the NRA, that everyone is safer with some cold hard steel—but let's not bother to add an unwarranted political slant to this film, though. **TERRORVISION** is pure camp fun and it's pretty much an '80s explosion of aliens, overly saturated colors and wackiness, which are all the elements that work to its advantage.

MONSTER IN THE CLOSET

Reviewed by Jason "Skunkape" Cook

USA, 1986. D: Bob Dahlin

Ad-line: *"It's Out! It's Out! It's Out!"*

Narration from Troma's US trailer: *"The most mysterious, inexplicable and incredible events often take place in the most ordinary places. Usually these seemingly unexplainable occurrences are eventually explained. But, every so often, they remain mysteriously incredible... Yes, it was something so hideous, so gruesome, so frightful that it could only dwell in one place: among the slippers and pajamas in the grisly depths of your* closet! *The entire United States Marine Corps could not stop it! The most sophisticated armored weaponry and firepower could* not *stop it! Fantastic cinematic special effects could* not *stop it! The most highly-developed nuclear flowerpots could* not *stop it! Even the most incredible array of international superstars could* not *stop it! ...It's gripping, it's shocking, it's horrifying! Was it a deranged killer, or was it just looking for a* date? *...MONSTER IN THE CLOSET: it's coming out!"*

MITC is a PG-rated monster movie with no blood, pretty much no bad language, and no sex; none other than Lloyd Kaufman and Michael Herz's company Troma released it on home video. It may seem strange based on their reputation for putting out mostly juvenile filth (which I love!), that Troma would distribute something without an R rating. Do not dismiss it based on rating alone, however, because it does deliver a few hearty laughs and a cool-looking creature. This movie is a Troma acquisition rather than an in-house production, so it doesn't take place in Tromaville, NJ. Still, it did get slightly Tromatized in postproduction, but none of their trademark gore or green slime was added; just an additional voiceover from Kenneth Kessler, who also provided Toxie's voice in the mother of all Troma movies, Herz & Kaufman's **THE TOXIC AVENGER** (1984, USA). When the title monster herein lures an unsuspecting victim inside the closet, all the viewer gets to see and hear are clothes flying out, along with screams and growls. It's pretty damn hilarious every time! This film is all about the comedy, but sadly, as entertaining as it may be, it's definitely not always funny. Throughout the movie, text appears on the screen letting us know what the time and day is, no matter how irrelevant. This gets old pretty quickly and becomes annoying.

Aside from a few hardcore fans of **MITC**, it has pretty much lurked in the shadows. If you didn't see it on shelves at the video store back in the '80s, you may have first heard of it around 2009 when **THE FAST AND THE FURIOUS** was raking in the dough at the box office. That's because the child star of the film is none other than Paul Walker, future second banana of the lunkhead Vin Diesel *F&F* series. Here he plays a boy genius named "The Professor". This discovery gave the film some buzz on the Internet, and I even remember seeing Walker on *The Tonight Show*. That night, Jay Leno showed a clip from **MITC**. I can't quote Leno exactly, but he did say something along the lines of "just how stupid the monster looked." Not sure how he has the balls to dis anything film-related: I mean, did anyone see him and Pat Morita in Lewis Teague's **COLLISION COURSE** (1989, USA)? But, the monster is *supposed* to look silly! It has a big brown body with a hunchback, very tiny eyes, and a mouth that won't close. The mouth resembles the Sarlac Pit from **RETURN OF THE JEDI** (you know, the huge thing out in the desert that will slowly digest you for over a thousand years). Inside is another little head that pops out and bites its victims vampire-style, leaving two tiny teeth marks on all their lifeless bodies. The special effects team really came through, bringing something special to this low budget movie. It's goofy, but interesting to look at every time it's on screen. But before I forget, Paul Walker isn't the only childhood actor to appear in this film. The third closet victim, a little girl playing hide and go seek, is none other than Fergie from the Black Eyed Peas! She only has a small role, because once she's in the closet, it's "Boom Boom Pow", and then she's gone.

The writer/director is Bob Dahlin, who really never directed another feature film after this one. He does however have an impressive résumé as a first and second assistant director. For instance, he was the 1st AD on Robert Altman's **POPEYE** (1980, USA). This job is what may have helped him get two of Popeye's veteran actors for the film: Paul Dooley, who played Wimpy, is a victim of the closet monster here, and Donald Moffat, who was the tax collector of Sweethaven, plays an Army general hell-bent on destroying the monster. The cast also includes John Carradine, Claude Akins and Howard Duff, but stay tuned, as there are plenty more familiar faces to come; in fact you could fill up all 9 Hollywood Squares and still have a few celebrities left over for guest appearances on *Fantasy Island*, or even *The Love Boat*!

So, as I said before, this movie does not take place in Tromaville, NJ; it takes place in the small, quiet college town of Chestnut Hills, CA. Richard Clark (Donald Grant), who writes obituaries for the local paper, asks his boss for a chance to do something bigger. The paper's hotshot reporter is aptly nicknamed "Scoop" (Frank Ashmore), but you may know him better as **AIRPLANE**'s "What's our vector, Victor?" bit-player. Scoop finds an article about the closet murders in a trashcan. His boss and the reporter give Richard this assignment, not realizing that it will soon become the biggest story of the century. Richard begins his investigation at the local sheriff's office; that's where he meets the young Professor (Walker) and his mom, Diane (Denise DuBarry). Diane is a scientist who has some theories about these inexplicable deaths, and is sharing them with the police. She is also a health nut, and things get off on the wrong foot when our hero gives her son a Nestlé's Crunch bar. All is soon forgiven, because, when Richard's "Clark Kent"-style glasses fall off, she becomes mesmerized—frozen in time, if you will—and falls in love with that handsome mug of his. Things really get interesting when Diane's boss, the scientific head of the university, gets involved. It's *Laugh-In*'s Henry Gibson—Mr. "**THE 'BURBS**" himself—giving us his patented "strange deadpan weird guy" performance, played to perfection, as Dr. Pennyworth. Together they record audio from the latest closet attack and believe that, with a series of musical notes, they can communicate with this creature (shades of Spielberg's **CLOSE ENCOUNTERS OF THE THIRD KIND** [1977, USA]!). The jingle does indeed manage to lure the monster out of the closet, and before the military can start blasting away at it, Dr. Pennyworth steps out in front of them with his trusty xylophone. Just when there's some hope that the monster can be reasoned with, he kills the poor scientist. Guns are shot and missiles are fired, but nothing seems to work. With the whole world in a panic, our heroes believe that maybe electrocuting it will suck out

Spanish poster for **MONSTER IN THE CLOSET**. The same artwork was seen on American posters (artist unknown)

its energy...but that plan fails big-time. The electrical trap is destroyed, it seems all is lost, and, just when the monster is about to kill Richard, his glasses are knocked off, whereupon the monster also becomes captivated by his stunning good looks, and promptly falls in love with him. The big brown beast then picks up Richard and carries him back into the closet unharmed. You see, this movie might just be considered one big gay joke: as in monster comes "out of the closet" (get it?). In the end, it will be beauty that kills the beast, and—believe it or not—that famous line from **KONG** is actually stolen and reused in this film!

Having become enamored of the film's hunky hero (Donald Grant), **MITC**'s lovesick monster—played by 6' 9" Kevin Peter Hall, who also played the Predator—carts him off...to the closet!

So, how do you stop this thing? You must destroy every closet, and so everyone in the entire world is ordered to axe or burn them up! This forces the monster out yet again, but—*oops!*—one last closet has been forgotten, and, with the monster's energy rapidly dwindling, he's got one last chance to get himself and his newfound love to safety. Can the beast get the beauty back inside that one remaining closet and live happily ever after…?

MONSTER IN THE CLOSET is a great way to spend an hour-and-a-half. My only real complaint is Barrie Guard's terrible, generic score (and, alas, I did also say there is no sex), but there is some good news, if you were at least expecting a little T&A! There's a Stella Stevens shower scene, and those boobs come into frame just long enough to put a smile on anyone's face…except for maybe the monster's, of course!

ALIEN LOCKDOWN
(a.k.a. **CREATURE**)

Reviewed by Christos Mouroukis

USA, 2004. D: Tim Cox

Ad-line: *"They Needed Alien DNA to Make a Weapon. Now they'll need a Miracle to Survive."*

The first thing that got my attention about his flick—as is often the case—was the synopsis. This time the one at *imdb.com*, from which I was told that: *"…a team of commandos is sent into a genetic*

research lab and end up getting stalked by a creature that looks a lot like the Predator". That's all you need to know, basically. I was sold. But then I thought, maybe the person who wrote it has not seen anything more obscure than **PREDATOR** (1987, USA), and so possibly his description of the monster was a bit irrelevant. Maybe the monster would be something greater, or—even better— something worse![1] But the guy was spot-on; dude in the suit looks a lot like the alien from the aforementioned Arnold Schwarzenegger classic, and this is made clear very early on as the creature wastes no time and attacks a bunch of scientists, leaving a slaughterhouse behind it. Is this bad? Hell no, it's fucking A-class entertainment! I got the perfect flick, I got the pizzas, I got the booze; now, where are the strippers? (Oh, I forgot, this is a night in, and girls don't like my cheap-ass apartment...)

The film is basically about a meteor that crashes on Earth many thousands of years ago and leaves a magical green stone behind it, which for a while is used by soldiers during wars throughout history because it gives them superpowers and they win every battle. I may make this sound a bit cheesy, but wait until you hear the narrator. Anyway, said stone was lost in time. Now it is discovered by a corrupted archaeologist who arranged it to give it to the man he's taking orders from, who in turn wants it in order to become more powerful…and that's where your creature problems begin, right there.

---

[1] Er, there's no telling how much I like bad-looking monsters… On the other hand, I write for *Monster!*, so maybe there *is* telling…

A toothy grin is all this monster has during its ALIEN LOCKDOWN

This is a very fascinating movie, and the CGI when used actually looks great. This was premiered on the Sci-Fi Channel (in February 2004)[2] so I'll assume that you know the special effects I am giving praise about are not anything like **TRANSFORMERS** (2007, USA), but I also believe that you didn't come here to read about Michael Bay either. The box cover screams *"I ripped-off ALIEN's sequels"*, but our readers are not that easily fooled. This was shot in Sofia, Bulgaria, where films are made for cheap, so you should know what you're getting yourself into.

The creature is pretty much kept in shadows throughout most of the film's running time, but even when you get glimpses of it, it's nothing less than *awesome*! When you see it in the clear, the thing looks fantastic! So honestly, this is not a movie about Shakespearian performances, but believe me, the actors did their best. These include James Marshall (**A FEW GOOD MEN** [1992, USA][3]), Michelle Goh (**OUT FOR A KILL** [2003, Aruba/USA]), John Savage (you don't need an introduction for this guy, he's the picture's "name attraction", and you should go watch him in **THE GODFATHER: PART III** [1990, USA], etc.), as well as Martin Kove (**RAMBO: FIRST BLOOD PART II** [1985] and **THE KARATE KID, PART II** [1986, both USA]).

Tim Cox, who directed this, has had a very interesting career. He directed a couple of short films from 1998 to 2001, and he also worked in music videos and commercials and on **THE MARRIAGE UNDONE** (2002, USA) as a

camera assistant. As a director he made his feature-length TV-movie debut with the film under review here, which was followed by **LARVA** (a.k.a. **MORPHMAN**, 2005, USA/Germany) starring William Forsythe, **MAMMOTH** (2006, USA/Romania) starring Tom Skerritt, and **MISS NOBODY** (2010, USA) starring Leslie Bibb. He also co-wrote **KRAKEN: TENTACLES OF THE DEEP** (2006, USA/Canada) starring Christa Campbell, and **GRYPHON** (2007, USA) starring Jonathan LaPaglia. Stay tuned, because it looks like I might review more of his stuff for some future issue of *Monster!*

AMERICAN WARSHIPS
(a.k.a. AMERICAN BATTLESHIP)

Reviewed by Christos Mouroukis

USA, 2012. D: Thunder Levin

Ad-line: *"When Modern Weapons fail...It's Time to Bring in the Big Guns"*.

This film kicks off with a title card which tells us that, according to the US Department of Defence, what we are about to see actually never happened. When you know that this was made by The Asylum, and for only $1,000,000, don't you suspect that with such a claim at the beginning you're in for a whole lot of crap? Yes, me too; and crap is indeed what we'll get.

Planes fall straight into the sea, and a ship is getting bombarded, until the US forces start believing

---

2 It was released on disc in 2005.
3 Now, that is a great title for a parody! You know of which kind...

they are under attack by the Asians (either Korean, or Chinese, or both—it doesn't matter, discrimination makes no discriminations). But, no matter how hard **AMERICAN BATTLESHIP** is trying to be a War picture—there are shootouts between ships, between aircraft, and pretty much any kind of firepower you can think of—it is in actuality a monster movie. You see, the ones that are responsible for the attacks are...*aliens*! Yes, monstrous, ugly motherfuckin' aliens!

Now, these aliens resemble a combination between an old man and a fish (think of medusas in particular), and they also have the ability to shoot fire with—*er*—their flamethrowers. If you know what you're getting into (meaning, considering the production house and the low budget), you can forgive the way the CGI aliens look, but I promise you, you will never forget the idea behind them. I mean, who in their right mind designed aliens like these?! It's nice for our monsters to be unique from time to time, but these are plain silly.

This is a rip-off of Peter Berg's **BATTLESHIP** (2012, USA), which I have not seen, and I don't plan to. It was originally called **AMERICAN BATTLESHIP**, but Universal Studios slammed a copyright lawsuit on The Asylum in regards to the title, and so it was renamed **AMERICAN WARSHIPS** instead.

AMERICAN WARSHIPS was written and directed by Thunder Levin. Mr. Levin's directorial debut is **MUTANT VAMPIRE ZOMBIES FROM THE 'HOOD!** (2008). He has written **200 M.P.H.** (2011) and **ATLANTIC RIM** (2013, all USA). He also directed **AE: APOCALYPSE EARTH** (2013, USA). He is mostly known as the screenwriter of all three films (so far) in the *Sharknado* franchise (2013 to the present). I love the *Sharknado*s, especially for their outrageous humour, but they have been reviewed to death, so stay tuned and I will review the other titles for some future issue of *Monster!*

This film was line-produced by Chris Ray, who is of course Fred Olen Ray's son. I plan on writing a big-ass piece on the films of Chris Ray, because he is a great filmmaker in his own right, but this will happen after I finish my series of articles on legendary F.O. Ray's filmography for *Weng's Chop*. (Damn, did I just reveal something?)

As I assume you know, The Asylum's films are not about Oscar-winning performances, but you often see familiar faces from the B-movie world. This time around we get: Mario Van Peebles (Melvin Van Peebles' son), Carl Weathers (**PREDATOR**

[1987]), hottie Johanna Watts (**IN MEMORIUM** {*sic*} [2005]), and Nikki McCauley (**KARLA** [2006], all USA).

You don't need to purchase this, by any means. If you absolutely must see every Asylum film that is out there, find a way for this one that will cost you absolutely zero money. Maybe a friend has it on DVD and wants you to watch it with him/her? Although I wouldn't be so sure if he/she really is your friend for putting you through this and all.

Don't get me wrong, I'm not angry with the film. In fact, I believe that we should embrace its business model. Films made for around $1,000,000 are like the middle class, which the economy wants to wipe from the face of the Earth. Pretty much like what happens with the whole Western Crisis now: you know, the rich getting richer and the poor becoming poorer. The film business is now full of no-budget independent flicks and then the gazillion-dollar crapfests. These types of monster movies are celluloid's middle class, and that's why we should keep on supporting them.

DEADLY EYES
(a.k.a. **THE RATS**)

Reviewed by Dennis Capicik

Canada, 1982. D: Robert Clouse

Blu-ray ad-line: *"Tonight, they will rise from the darkness beneath the cities...to feed!"*

Beginning with a lecture, university professor Dr. Spenser (Cec Linder) dishes out facts about the common rat or *rattus rattus* to a group of disinterested high school "kids", who look more like they're in their late-twenties. "There are 24 rats to every man, woman and child today", he says. "In our country alone, they will destroy over 1 billion dollars of property annually and consume one fifth of food crops planted. So why is our war on the rat being lost?" Dr. Spenser ponders this question but doesn't get much of a response, because Trudy (Lisa Langlois) and her friends (including Lesleh Donaldson) have their eyes set on Paul Harris (Sam Groom), their high school teacher whose "animal" inside him is apparently just "waiting to escape".

Meanwhile, Kelly Leonard (Sara Botsford), a rather scrupulous employee at the "Regional Department of Health" of this unnamed US City (in actuality, Toronto, Canada) continually clashes with her boss (James B. Douglas) due to his political aspirations. This time, she is overseeing the destruction of a vast shipment of corn that has become a health hazard because it's "infested with rodents" and "full of steroids". Along with her assistant George Foskins (Scatman Crothers), she orders the entire shipment to be burned, which, due to the steroids, unleashes a mutant strain of giant rats onto the populace. According to Dr. Spenser, rats are normally regarded as "scavengers and not hunters", but when George is found chewed to bits ("there wasn't much left") while investigating the sewer system, Sara conveniently meets Paul and the both of them try to convince city officials about the potential disaster.

In between the mayhem, Paul and Sara also manage to strike up a relationship, which at one point is seriously derailed when Trudy surprises our squeaky-clean hero with an impromptu visit to his bedroom clad in lacy red lingerie. For a brief moment, the film becomes a typical '80s teen comedy, but, unlike in many of those films, Trudy *does* keeps her clothes on here.

Using the sewer system as their "freeway", these "super rats" (portrayed by either Dachshunds in rat "costumes" [shades of **THE KILLER SHREWS**!] or animatronic puppets in close-ups) chomp on a few more people (including a toddler!) while low-angle POV shots dominate much of the action, until Sara is completely baffled when she exclaims, "I know everything there is to know about cockroaches, but I'm completely over my head on something like this". Due to the opening of a new subway line locally, all her superiors ignore her requests to deal with the ever-escalating and deadly rat problem the city is facing and, naturally enough, continue with the gala opening at "State Street Station" (actually TO's own "lost" lower Bay Street Station), but as in most of these nature-runs-amok flicks, you just *know* these nasty "little" critters are gonna crash the party!

Aside from the climactic siege along the new proposed subway line, one of the more memorable attacks occurs at the screening of a "Bruce Lee Retrospective" at the still-standing and still-operational Regent Theatre in Toronto. Taking its cue from Irving S. Yeaworth's **THE BLOB** (1958, USA), patrons run screaming from the theater as the mutated critters attack whomever they can sink their gnarly teeth into, and as for the theater, it looks pretty much exactly the same as it did 33 years ago.

Director Robert Clouse (1928-1997) was certainly an odd choice to helm this Canadian-lensed monster flick, which was co-financed by Golden Harvest, the production company out of Hong Kong who were also responsible for partially funding Clouse's seminal MA actioner **ENTER THE DRAGON** (1973, HK/USA). In fact, the print

Millionbyens rotter skriger af sult...
-de slår til overalt og de er flere end os!

KÆMPE·ROTTERNE ANGRIBER

De griber dig råt og hårdt i struben, -og slipper ikke, når filmen slutter...

SAM GROOM · SARA BOTSFORD · SCATMAN CROTHERS · CEC LINDER
INSTRUKTION ROBERT CLOUSE PRODUKTION JEFFERY SCHECHTMAN OG POUL KAHNERT MUSIK ANTHONY GUEFEN

German artwork for **DEADLY EYES**

supplied for Scream Factory's Blu-ray, under the bland title of **NIGHT EYES**, came courtesy of Fortune Star, as they currently hold the rights to most of the Golden Harvest film library. No doubt, Mr. Clouse was most likely hired because of his association with this once-prolific company. In an interesting bit of trivia, Clouse also directed the killer canine thriller **THE PACK** (1977, USA) a few years earlier, which featured a pack of abandoned dogs on an island getaway that terrorized a group of vacationers. According to the extras on the disc for the present title, Clouse wasn't too pleased working in the middle of winter, but he still manages to put together a fairly effective and fast-paced film, and, unlike the incredibly dark, three-decades old domestic VHS tape from Warner Home Video, René Verzier's photography comes through looking just fine, capturing a snowy Toronto with perfect accuracy; you can practically *feel* the chilly winter leap off the screen!

Both Sam Groom (born 1938) and Sara Botsford (1951-) continue to be prolific TV actors, with dozens upon dozens of credits on each of their IMDb profiles. Also in '82—the same year Botsford starred in **DEADLY EYES**—she appeared in another Canadian-lensed horror pic, Michael Anderson's **MURDER BY PHONE** (1982), a.k.a. **BELLS**, as it's more commonly known in Canada. **DE**'s costars Lisa Langlois (1959-) and Lesleh Donaldson (1964-) were also quite prolific in the early '80s Canadian horror boom, and both were also seen in J. Lee Thompson's slasher flick **HAPPY BIRTHDAY TO ME** (1981) the year before, while Langlois also appeared in Mark Lester's

strangely prophetic **CLASS OF 1984** (1982, Canada). As for Donaldson's Canuxploitation career, she also appeared in William Fruet's **FUNERAL HOME** (originally titled **CRIES IN THE NIGHT**, 1980) and Richard Ciupka's troubled production **CURTAINS** (1983). In **DE**, also look out for Canuck character actors Michael Fawkes and Roger Dunn as a train motorman and doctor, respectively.

Despite being based on James Herbert's pulp novel *The Rats* (I've never read it, so I can't comment on it; it was released on video in the UK under that title), **DEADLY EYES** works perfectly well as a modestly budgeted monster pic, and, in this era of flawless effects work and CGI, those effectively made-up Dachshunds and animatronic puppets are a great deal of fun, especially in this newest incarnation from Scream Factory. It's nice to finally have this Canadian creature feature back in circulation!

ANDROID APOCALYPSE
(a.k.a. **FACING EXTINCTION**)

Reviewed by Christos Mouroukis

USA/Canada, 2006. D: Paul Ziller

Ad-line: *"Yesterday, they wanted each other dead. Today, they need each other to survive".*

I did a lot of thinking in regards to reviewing this film for *Monster!*, because it is about androids, and some readers may feel that these are just robots (i.e., not monsters per se). But please allow me to elaborate. Androids are not totally machines, and they are certainly not entirely hu-

man, but they do have biology in them, so in my educated opinion these elements make them monsters. They were also originally created by human scientists, pretty much as in **FRANKENSTEIN** (1931, USA), the archetypical manmade monster movie.[4] The ones in this film are also bleeding green blood (unlike humans, who bleed red), so my case is strong enough. *[Indeed it is, Christos! Artificial humans definitely constitute monsters in M!'s criteria –Ed.]*

Now that you've gotten over the above, let's move on to this film, written by Karl Schiffman [**DEAD END** [1998, Canada]). It is set on a post-apocalyptic Earth, in which the resources are running out, and the titular creatures—which are actually of alien origin—have taken over and keep humans as slaves; kind of like in Victor Halperin's **WHITE ZOMBIE** (1932, USA), only here there is certain hierarchy among the robots and some of them are in power while others are programmed into doing hard labor. The latter resemble soldiers that take orders, but I guess there's really not much difference between the two.

The film focuses on the story of Jute (Scott Bairstow from **THE POSTMAN** [1997, USA]), a human being who is forced to do a lot of fighting (wrestling-style, which is awesome[5]; actually, all fight scenes are quite nicely staged). One day he takes his anger out on an android and manages to kill it. He is then tried and convicted for this murder, and the master race's cops get to kidnap his girlfriend, too. Along with a few other prisoners and their android guards they are travelling through the desert on their way to a high-security holding facility. This is when the mission gets attacked by flying robotic weapons of mass destruction, and this is the point when the film becomes too much of a **TERMINATOR SALVATION** (2009, USA/Germany/UK/Italy) kind of flick[6], but this doesn't last too long, as the whole affair is actually closer to the **BRAZIL** (1985, UK) or **TRANCERS** (1984, USA) territory. In fact, had this been a Charles Band production it would most likely be praised as some sort of *1984*ish masterpiece![7]

Anyway, after the hijacking incident the only survivors are Jute and his android guard DeeCee (Joseph Lawrence). There is a strange relationship growing between human and android here, one

---

4 And pretty much like that Dolly clone, which to me seemed like a monstrous experiment.

5 Your favorite WWE star Chris Jericho has a bit part.

6 Even though it was made three years before, but then again, the whole thing can remind you a bit of **TERMINATOR 2: JUDGMENT DAY** (1991, USA); you get the idea.

7 Yes. I mean George Orwell!

could even say with homosexual undertones, but maybe it is just friendship. The two are bound together by a seemingly unbreakable handcuff-like steel string (*er*, sexual fantasy?). You see, the protagonist just wants his freedom and tries to fight for it, but then he is forced to work with the android, who/which he convinced that, rather than going together to the Terminus where they could break free of each other but still be slaves to the machine, they instead head towards Phoenix to live like men. And speaking of men, this was actually broadcasted under the aegis of the *movies-4men* banner (I'd call them *movies4semen*!).

Jokes aside, this is a very exciting movie—full of explosions and such action—that you should not miss. Even if you are a film snob, you can pretend this was made 20 years before by Italians (maybe Bruno Mattei?), and you'll still be cool with yourself. It cost $1,000,000 to make and it looks as if most of it got to the screen, Roger Corman-style.

Paul Ziller, who directed this, has a very interesting career in television. He used to wear many hats, but he now spends most of his professional life directing TV movies such as **BEYOND LOCH NESS** (2008, Canada). Certainly, it doesn't look like he'll win an Oscar any time soon, but he is a guarantee-stamp for outrageous entertainment…and that's all you need, basically, for a night in.

THE LAST FRANKENSTEIN

(ラスト・フランケンシュタイン / *Rasuto Furankenshutain*)

Reviewed by Eric Messina

Japan, 1991. D: Takeshi Kawamura

Lately I've suffered through a bunch of shitty Frankenstein movies, and **FRANKENSTEIN GENERAL HOSPITAL** (1988, USA) springs to mind as a particularly atrocious nightmare trying to pass itself off as comedy. There are just too many to mention; the Boris Karloff/ Mary Shelley staple has been passed through the cinematic meat grinder of history. **THE LAST FRANKENSTEIN** is an early '90s Japanese take on the legend with semi-interesting results. I had some high expectations, considering that I just reviewed **FRANKENSTEIN CONQUERS THE WORLD** (1965) and **THE WAR OF THE GARGANTUAS** (1966, two epic monster mashes *[which Eric reviewed in* Monster! *issues #11 and 12, respectively –ed]* from the land of Hiroshima mutant casualties and delicious sushi. I originally tracked this film down to be reviewed on my site Theater of Guts (*theaterofguts.com*), since it was featured in Chas. Balun's VHS bootleg catalog. However, I decided to bring it over to

THE LAST FRANKENSTEIN pics –
Top: Quentin Tarantinostein! **Center:** "For chrissakes, get my agent on the phone!" **Above:** The Fundies' separation surgery was a success! *[Custom captions c/o Erok "Crankenstein" Hellhammer]*

On the streets of Tokyo, we see a death-fixated religious cult, and the media (who are unusually chipper) mention how an epidemic of suicide is becoming more popular than ever! In reality back during the '90s when the national economy tanked, it triggered mass suicides in Japan. According to the BBC's Andrew Harding, there are currently suicide chat rooms online for partners looking to find someone else to join them, and it seems like there's an epidemic of depression with no psychiatric help in sight. The article mentions how they are trying to deter people from jumping off station platforms onto the tracks in front of oncoming trains, so at least that's kind of helpful. In the woods of Mount Fuji, there's a notorious suicide spot called Aokigahara, around that area, and there are road signs telling those who visited there to end it all that they should possibly reconsider. Yeah, that's right: **THE LAST FRANKEN-STEIN** is a real uplifting film, let me tell you!

During Professor Surusawa's pathology class, he is challenged by one of his nerdy female students. She believes that social pressure has more impact on the human body than other factors discussed in class. During this debate, there's a dead naked female on the teacher's desk (the cadaver is later stolen for Aleo's "Bride of Frankenstein"). The teacher, who is played by Akira Emoto, is a total dick, and instead of engaging in a mature conversation with his student, he humiliates her in front of an entire packed classroom. Later on, he has sex with the same student as they continue to wonder why the suicide rate is so astronomical. Maybe that scenario was part of their roleplaying? Each section of the film flashes to a computer screen, which illustrates how the professor is working on documenting what happens over the course of the film.

The suicide cult members all wear white face makeup and seem to always be lurking in the background; they yell things like "Worship Death!" The Doctor is definitely crazy, and sees a floating doll that greets him at the door. The filmmakers take all sorts of liberties with the Frankenstein theme and pepper it with tons of depression; it's basically a doom-driven reinterpretation of the tale…which wasn't exactly that uplifting to begin with.

There's a theologian think-tank that is chockfull of some of Tokyo's least funny comedians (one guy dresses like Col. Sanders!), and they all scoff at how suicide is the new social disease sweeping the nation. The ridiculous staff all mention Dr. Aleo, whom they believe went insane and should definitely not be sought out by the professor character. The way the men behave made me think that insanity is more of a contagious disease than depression. I like the message of one doctor, who says that disposable fads are becoming more im-

the readers of *Monster!* instead. Balun was always ahead of his time, and has introduced me to some of the most disgusting, outrageous and insane films from Hong Kong. He described this Japanese film as "ambitious, with pustule-popping plagues and corpse-snatchin' hunchbacks" to look forward to… so what's not to like?!

The film opens with a doomy quote by Akira Aleo, about how humanity will live longer only to complain more. If that doesn't raise your spirits, there's that always-effective public domain bumout song "Moonlight Sonata" by Beethoven to set you off on a "sadgasm". Later on, we discover that Aleo is the Dr. Frankenstein of this story.

portant in society, which are causing the rampant suicides. The same man later shoots himself while surrounded by three live chickens who "ham" it up for the camera (I thought they were funnier than the terrible comedians in the theology scene!).

A hunchback, played by Naomasa Musaka, drives dead bodies around in a VW Bug. He shows up and punches Sarusawa in a wacky boxing scene complete with a novelty "Ding" sound. The white-faced corpses seen in the back of his car look as if the hunchback and Aleo are murdering the suicide cult for experimental subjects. Then the film switches back to show more student fatalities (I wonder if the pressure of keeping up their grades is contributing to the suicide rate?).

Sarusawa's daughter Mai, has powers of levitation, which were brought on by the trauma of her mother's suicide. Dr. Aleo (Yoshio Harada)—who wears a killer eye-patch and trench coat and looks like a Captain Harlock/Snake Plissken hybrid—finally shows up and greets the protagonist of this film. His wife is one of the most annoying characters I've ever seen in an Asian horror film!

Dr. Aleo has given up on the human race, and Sarusawa is disappointed that he has no interest in fixing the suicide problem. Instead, his plan is to reanimate two corpses (who wear handy-dandy jockstraps over their genitals) with psychic powers and make them procreate as the new "Adam and Eve". The main character was only chosen because his daughter possesses the ability to bring Dr. Aleo a.k.a. Frankenstein's creations to life.

The actors who play the monster and his bride are just awful. Once Mai brings them to life, they inevitably become withdrawn and frustrated, just like you'd expect. When you watch a Japanese Frankenstein monster movie and are not impressed by the creature, it's a bad sign of a weak film. **THE LAST FRANKENSTEIN** has a lot of great elements that just don't fit together properly, and the pacing is exhausting. Although I did really like the spooky-fetus-in-a-jar-that-jostles-around-in-the-attic moment: maybe he should've had his own movie!

The film has a strange mix of unfunny comedy and philosophical mumbo jumbo, which make it watchable, but its worst crime is that it's very tedious and annoying. It seriously could use some rewrites and editing (the film doesn't really get moving until the second hour). Some critics, like *Shock Cinema*'s Steven Puchalski, have compared it to Cronenberg. I see where he's coming from, but felt that Kawamura also attempts to be an Asian Mel Brooks, with unsatisfying results. If only the film had just stuck to one genre, then it would've been more successful as a solid, original

take on the Frankenstein mythos. I felt that it was entertaining enough, but too uneven in its execution, and the comedy was wildly out of place.

NOTE: For more about Japan's internet "suicide clubs", visit *http://news.bbc.co.uk/2/hi/programmes/newsnight/4071805.stm*

THE DEADLY SPAWN
(a.k.a. RETURN OF THE ALIEN'S DEADLY SPAWN)

Reviewed by Matt Bradshaw

USA, 1983, D: Douglas McKeown

Narration from 21st Century Film Corporation's US trailer: *"First there was the INVASION OF THE BODYSNATCHERS. Then there was ALIEN. Now there is THE DEADLY SPAWN! It began with a meteor crashing to Earth. No one knew the mystery of the mutant spores it contained. Now...they are free! They will grow and reproduce rapidly, eating anything and anyone in their path. THE DEADLY SPAWN: the nightmare is just beginning! ...What do you do when unknown terror surrounds you? What do you do when there is no escape, nowhere to hide from being eaten alive? THE DEADLY SPAWN: they just keep multiplying like demon seed! THE DEADLY SPAWN: ex-*

THE DEADLY SPAWN: definitely made by film nerds

*traterrestrial terror! They're full of surprises, and the best is yet to come! Can anything stop these strange creatures? ...The movie real science fiction fans have been waiting for: **THE DEADLY SPAWN** want you to see them at this theater soon. They need every person they can get!"*

As with many horror flicks of the 1980s, my first glimpse of **THE DEADLY SPAWN**, and the three-headed beastie the film is built around, was in the pages of *Fangoria*. It looked cool enough, and the magazine showed off some pretty awesome effects, but finding and watching a film in

those days often wasn't as easy as it is today. Theatrical releases could be spotty, and even when it was released on tape, home video was for renting, not buying, so I was at the mercy of what was available in local rental shops. It was a few years yet before I finally tracked down a copy, and by then it was sporting the alternate title **RETURN OF THE ALIEN'S DEADLY SPAWN**. The idea there was to make casual renters think this was part of the *Alien* franchise, while I myself wondered if this was actually a sequel to **THE DEADLY SPAWN** rather than the original.

Chief technician Greg Ra-moundas with the "Mama" monster on the set of **THE DEADLY SPAWN**

I popped that bad boy into the VCR, adjusted the tracking, hiked up my leg warmers (a guy's shins could get real cold back in the '80s!) and watched **THE DEADLY SPAWN** unspool… Right from the start when you hear the Theremin-laced theme music and the title card fades into view with a nice ripply effect, you know the filmmakers had a love for the B monster movies of the 1950s. A little later when the first bucket of blood hits the wall, you know they were also looking to make an '80s-style gorefest. Producer Ted A. Bohus and his team nicely meld the sensibilities of the two decades in question, giving us a fun—though far from perfect—horror gem of the VHS/Beta era.

Two conspicuously nameless campers see a meteor fall to Earth near their campsite and decide to investigate. I say conspicuous because one of them repeatedly says "*Hey!*" to the other without ever addressing him by name. Perhaps it's best that we don't get too attached, though, since these two quickly become a midnight snack for the alien life-form that hitched a ride with the meteorite.

The next morning, it's raining cats and dogs (yet, sadly, no one steps in a poodle). The as-yet-unseen creatures take up residence in the dank basement of a family dwelling. It's not clear if there was more than one monster in that meteor, but by the next morning we find that these things reproduce like *bunnies*. Slimy, carnivorous, extraterrestrial bunnies! The majority are toothsome tadpoles of varying sizes, but the big mama alien is a three-headed monstrosity that, quite frankly, looks like a trio of giant penises with more teeth than an Osmond Family Christmas special.

Sam (James L. Brewster) and Barbara (Elissa Neil)—whose house the slimy critters have moved into—are the first to go, when a casual trip to the basement goes horribly awry for both. The first kills are nicely shot, with lots of quick cuts reminiscent of the shower scene in **PSYCHO** (believe it or not), and the decidedly unHitchcockian shot of Barbara's face being ripped-off is especially effective.

As the pair were expected to leave the house early that day, the rest of the family fails to notice them missing. Aunt Millie (Ethel Michelson) and Uncle Herb (John Schmerling) are visiting, in part so the head-shrinking uncle can provide psychoanalysis for 13-year-old Charles (Charles George Hildebrandt), who has a passion for scary movies and costumes, and his parents are a touch worried about this. How can a healthy mind be so passionate about that sort of stuff? Charles' older brother Pete (Tom DeFranco) has some friends coming over too; all of which provides a lovely in-house smorgasbord for the eating machines currently growing in the basement. Charles soon realizes

US newspaper ad

what's going on, though, and his encyclopedic knowledge of monsters is put to good use trying to quell the alien invasion.

According to producer Ted A. Bohus' commentary on the Elite Entertainment "Millennium Edition" Blu-ray, the total budget for the film was a mere $19,000. Even by early 1980s standards that's a pretty astoundingly low figure, made even more-so by the fact that the film works pretty well and features some good and occasionally outstanding creature effects. The acting is dodgy at times, not all of the effects can be called a complete success (the camera lingers far too long on that severed head, ruining the believability) but the pace is

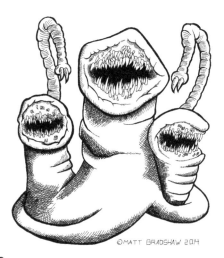

©MATT BRADSHAW 2014

Tim Hildebrandt clowns around behind-the-scenes on **THE DEADLY SPAWN**

steady, and the viewer is never bored. The movie also features some surprisingly detailed miniatures during the opening of the film and for the shock ending, which were designed by Tim Hildebrandt. Hildebrandt was one half of the fantasy art team of The Brothers Hildebrandt, whose many works include the original **STAR WARS** theatrical poster. Tim also allowed the film to be shot in his home (from what I hear, that's never a good idea) and even got his son to play Charles, its juvenile protagonist (his real-life dad played a doctor seen at the end of the film).

Apparently the production was plagued by creative differences. Director Douglas McKeown and effects coordinator John Dods butted heads so badly that Bohus felt it was endangering the film. As Dods was one of his original partners on the project, Bohus fired McKeown after most, but not all, of the film had been shot. Bohus' side of the story can be heard in the Blu-ray's commentary, as well as in a separate commentary recorded for a previous DVD release. To hear McKeown's take on things, I highly recommend reading Stephen Thrower's excellent book *Nightmare USA: The Untold Story of the Exploitation Independents* (FAB Press, 2007). The chapter on McKeown and **THE DEADLY SPAWN** is a fascinating read, and he goes into detail about the differences between what he had intended and what ended up in the final film. You can also hear an interview with the director on the *Junk Food Dinner* podcast (*http://www.junkfooddinner.com*), episode #98.

As I said, not a masterpiece, but it is a rollicking gore-filled product of its time, probably best viewed with a few friends and several beers.

FLIGHT TO HELL
(*Volo per l'inferno*)

Reviewed by Adam Parker-Edmondston

Italy, 2003. D: "Al Passeri" (Massimiliano Cerchi)

The "so bad it's good" tag for movies is thrown around quite a lot these days. Some films warrant the attention this tag creates, some do not. Sometimes just being a badly-made movie does not make for an entertaining film viewing experience. For fans of "these" movies—and we are many—you can instantly tell if a movie is going to fit into this category or not. Heck, I don't even like using the term, personally; whether a film is entertaining or not is all that matters to me, and if that comes from unintentional humor, then so be it!

Now, we all know the old favorites, such as **TROLL 2, MICROWAVE MASSACRE, PLAN 9 FROM OUTER SPACE, MANOS: THE HANDS OF FATE, THE BEAST OF YUCCA FLATS** and **THE ROOM**. The thing all these and a lot of movies of this "type" have in common is that the reason they are so incredible is not because of any failures in the script, acting, etc. departments (though all this helps). No, it is that they all have *heart*. Someone, somewhere wanted to make a good movie and—by jingo!—in their own way, they did. Now, one film that covers all these criteria, but fails to get on any of these lists is a 2003 Italian film which even then must have looked dated. I would like to introduce you all to this incredible guilty pleasure: ladies and gentlemen, I now present…**FLIGHT TO HELL**!

The start of the movie gives us a good indication of the oddness that is soon to follow. We zoom into an obviously distressed looking gentleman's eyeball, his pulsating retina showing us horrors yet to come. The dream is so intense that he soon awakens from it. The man in question is a pilot, and he needs to get his ass in gear because he is late for work!

Now, there is an important thing to note about the characters in **FLIGHT TO HELL**. They very rarely get mentioned by name, almost as if they never needed one anyway. IMDb struggled to get the names for characters, and only has two listed. But not to worry, I have included a helpful guide to some of the names I could pick up through countless viewings of the movie, together with a handy description of their not so well-drawn characters:

Don – The Captain
Pat – The crap female second captain/copilot
Bob – Short-haired, horny plane technician
Jack – Long-haired, less horny plane technician
Jen – Slutty hostess
Carol – Non-slutty hostess
David – Senator (or some other high-powered individual)
Mike – The jerk who is in charge of looking after the guests

There is an older guest on the plane with his bit on the side, but the poor guy hardly even gets a mention and his companion gets even less screen time, so I have no idea what they are called. One of the consorts has an outrageous accent. I think it is meant to be either Scottish or Irish, but your guess is as good as mine with regards to *what* they were playing! It's a sad state of affairs when a character—even one with a silly accent—is given so little screen attention that I forget who they even are.

Anyway back to the story: Don finally makes it to work at Roulette 1, the state-of-the-art gambling plane. It's not long before we get the characteri-

zation out of the way, with Bob trying to rape Jen, who, after her sexual taunting of him gets him horny, decides that the best course of action should be to let him into her knickers anyway. Not really sure what part of raping someone is found to be sexy, but that is the *least* of this film's worries; it's probably more disturbing that there is a *Carry On*-style vibe to the whole thing. Pat falls asleep at the helm of the plane while Don is in the can, meaning she misses the warning from the control office of a weird green cloud coming their way. The ship flies into it and some top quality *Star Trek*-style shenanigans ensue as the crew fall about all over the place. The green cloud in question looks very familiar. Even after using the freeze-framing feature, I am still not sure, but I could swear they have taken a scene out of Ridley Scott's **ALIEN** (1979) or James Cameron's **ALIENS** (1986, both USA/UK) and very briefly mixed it into the green cloud footage, resulting in an odd mishmash in the sky. So, everything is soon put back in order when Captain Don comes back, and, aside from a few pockets of green slime emerging on the ship, it seems to be business as usual.

Jen (on a rare occasion when she is not dishing out sexual references or getting laid) ends up slipping on some green slime after getting all excited about seeing a fancy dog cage in the cargo bay (don't ask!). The slime infects her, leading to it somehow incubating *something* in her knee. She manages to still stay slutty after this event, though, so do not panic. While she recovers, the rest of the passengers get to shagging. All the while the green slime begins spreading around the plane. Jen starts to get extreme hallucinations which cause her face to warp and also makes her see monsters. The rest of the crew just laugh off her hysteria. Parts of the plane start to malfunction, putting the already stressed crew on tenterhooks. When Jack goes to the loading bay to sort out the landing gear, he stumbles across some weird eggs (I can only assume the ones we saw at the start in the cloud); one of which shoots up into his nose, leaving a tentacle hanging out, in an un-intentionally hilarious scene.

The crew figure out that there are—yes!—creatures onboard, and it is these creatures which are eating the plane's internal workings, causing it to malfunction…meaning they will soon be up a certain creek without a paddle if they do not do something about it. The passengers however are oblivious, still going about their whoring and gambling ways. The crew decide to search the plane, looking for these creatures before they can do more damage, and manage to kill one of them (which look like a cross between a spider and a

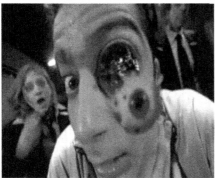

Xenomorph facehugger). Shades of **JAWS**, Mike merely buries his head in the sand, carrying on as though nothing bad is happening. Jack wakes from having the thing up his nose, while Bob goes egg hunting. He finds them, but they have all hatched and one (somehow) has turned into a massive, multi-limbed beast which pretty much devours Bob whole. Then it's Jack's turn, and, much like in **ALIEN**, his dining scene is interrupted by a creature erupting from his eye socket! Pat stalks the lower cabins with a blowtorch, trying to find the creature, and while this is going on one of the baby creatures attacks the crew and passengers while they are playing golf, but is quickly chased off. Following this, a new creature appears which Jen vomits forth, killing her in the process. The older passenger and his squeeze have been murdered by the creatures which now surround all the cabins. David gets a hole poked through his head via a creature's tail. As a last resort , the crew decide to blast the creatures into the air by blowing a hole in the side of the ship. Mike sabotages the plane for no reason other than he wants to sell the creatures. He threatens the crew with dynamite if they do not comply. When this fails, he takes the parachutes. The huge creature returns, taking out Mike and infecting him, turning him into a black-faced tentacle creature. With most of the crew now dead and one of the passengers actually being an alien it seems all is lost, and the plane shortly crashes at an undisclosed location. Seems the Don and Carol have survived and do not seem traumatized in the slightest by their experiences with the extraterrestrial killers. They even have time to share breakfast in the morning, as well as some sex (as they were too busy to do it on the plane like everyone else), but—alas for him—she is infected! The captain screams and we learn it has all only been a dream, after which he decides he is better off staying at home, and so he does!

You may notice that this film draws quite heavily from Ridley Scott's **ALIEN** (USA/UK, 1979) with regards to its plot and monsters. The parallels are easy to see with the facehugger-style creatures

---

Left: FLIGHT TO HELL pics *[from top to bottom]* – **How'd Dey Do Dat?!** Entry-level CG fuckery really runs rampant in this flippin' flick! **Top 2 pics:** An eye-popping scene which perhaps might lead you to believe that **FTH** was originally shot in 3D (it *wasn't*). **3rd pic:** Some digitally manipulated female facial distortions/contortions. No, her mouth isn't *really* that big! **Bottom:** "Third Eye Blind". If you'd just had a ginormous great hole blown clear through your head, you'd probably look just as surprised as this poor schmuck here does

infecting people, then those smaller creatures growing into bigger aliens being a prime example of this. But it gives the film a very weird feeling, because characters then randomly do things just so the action mimics those two movies. For example, when Mick decides to try and keep one of the creatures alive, it seems the only reason he wants to do it is because they did the exact same thing in **ALIEN**. Same with the use of flamethrowers (which is a pretty absurd thing to have on a plane, anyway). But the worst example of this slavish imitation comes when they substitute Ripley's cat for a dog and have it jump at a crew member in an out-of-the-blue-style "shock" scare!

Weird is the perfect word to describe this movie in general. A lot of the set is depicted by CGI; and not *good* CGI, either. It reminds me of the virtual reality scenes you would see in '90s science fiction movies, but the entire sets here are like this, as are all the games the passengers play. It gives the film a strange warped reality, because you know that none of what you are watching is real, because it's so badly CGI'd. In a way this sense of disconcertion works in the film's favor, giving it a bizarre reality all its own. It's almost like you are in a dream state, which seems kind of relevant when the "twist" ending is revealed. Now, I doubt this is intentional, but, if it is, then hats-off to the director.

The actors' performances seems very odd and off as well. Their stilted acting certainly doesn't help matters, but the fact that some of the actors are badly dubbed while some of them are not again adds to this overall feeling of strangeness. The bad acting does not seem to help the plot much, as their lack of emoting means quite serious stuff seems a lot less troublesome than you would imagine it would be in real life. Take for instant when the radio blows up, at which the pilot underreacts like it's a mere triviality, as though he has merely lost a pencil or forgotten to bring his lunch to work!

In keeping with the bad acting, this film delivers some of the most incredibly nonsensical dialogue I have ever heard delivered in a movie. For your delight, here are a few of my personal favorites:

"Batten down the hatches, here comes the weather!"
"Christ, what does he have up his nose?!"
"The radio is busted. We are going to have to land this sucker with no wheels, and Jack has a monster up his nose."
"This was supposed to be a joyride, but it is turning into a nightmare!"

But what you all really want to hear about is the creatures, right? Well, they are quite simply stun-

The notorious "parasite-wriggling-up-the-guy's-nose" scene from **FLIGHT TO HELL**

ning! I am guessing the giant creature is CGI-created, because it moves very oddly, almost like stop-motion. The smaller creatures are full on CGI creations, and are black, multi-legged things that when they pop up remind me of a warped version of the birds from James Nguyen's **BIRDEMIC: SHOCK AND TERROR** (2010, USA). The big creature is equipped with these weird appendages which it uses as arms, has an extremely huge mouth, and looks a little like a mutated piranha! It also resembles a cross between a Xenomorph and the creature from Roger Corman's **THE TERROR WITHIN** (1989, USA). It has "Predator"-vision, seeing only in greens and reds, and roars like a lion. The spider creatures that morph into this big one are incredibly funny, with one scene having the captain chase one about a golf course with a golf club, while it jerkily jumps around evasively and leaps onto people's faces. This scene goes on for a few minutes, with the captain seemingly killing it, then having it suddenly jump back up again! The creatures can go through walls, which conveniently helps in excusing the CGI problem of mapping the creatures' movements out on the screen correctly.

There are some other very strange errors in this flick, too. For instance, why does Jen vomit her creature out, rather than it bursting from her knee? That's where she was infected, and in Jack's case it came out roughly in the same area of infection. Also, how the heck did the slime infect her damn knee in the first place? Absorption through the skin, I imagine, but everyone else is infected differently. When Mike becomes infected, half his face turns black and he grows a fin! The crew seem to struggle while hunting for the big creature, but it sure finds them quick enough, and, on a plane so small, where is it possibly going to hide? Some scenes seem to have been left out entirely. The flamethrower segment seems to go nowhere,

"The Petrified City": Belgian poster for **THE MONOLITH MONSTERS** (art unsigned)

creature can shape-shift. No explanation is given, and, to be honest, this far into the movie you are so absorbed in the film's strange narrative that you will hardly question it either way.

These are just a handful of reason why I love this movie so much. Director Al Passeri (also known by the name Massimiliano Cerchi) has managed to craft either the most realistic portrayal of a fever dream ever caught on camera or one of the oddest movies in existence. It hardly matters, because once **FLIGHT TO HELL** has been absorbed into your temporal lobes, it is never to be forgotten. Al Passeri also directed another "Z" feature called **CREATURES FROM THE ABYSS** (*Creature dagli abissi*, a.k.a. **PLANKTON**, 1998, Italy [see *Monster!* #13]), this time with raping fish creatures attacking people on a boat! That too is an **ALIEN** rip-off and also seems strangely out-of-whack. Whether you've tired of the usual list of bad-good/good-bad movies, or if you just want to be entertained by a monster movie that, if nothing else, gives you a viewing experience you will never have had before, then **FLIGHT TO HELL** is just the ticket.

while other cast members drift in and out of the movie. I completely forgot about the older gentleman and his lady friend until they were shown getting murdered later on. The oddest thing out of the lot is the fact that suddenly the giant alien

THE MONOLITH MONSTERS

Reviewed by John Harrison

USA, 1957. D: John Sherwood

Criminally undervalued by many people when discussing the science fiction and horror cinema produced by Universal Studios throughout the 1950s, **THE MONOLITH MONSTERS** would have to rate as one of the true eclectic genre gems from that wondrous decade. True, it may not *quite* reach the heights of some other Universal classics from that period (such as Jack Arnold's trilogy of **CREATURE FROM THE BLACK LAGOON** [1954], **TARANTULA** [1955] and **THE INCREDIBLE SHRINKING MAN** [1957, all USA]), but it has a *frisson* and originality to it that is quite unique and impossible to resist.

Based on a story by Jack Arnold and Robert M. Fresco, **THE MONOLITH MONSTERS** takes place in fictional San Angelo, one of those wonderful, small Southern Californian desert towns which only seem to exist in 'Fifties fantasy cinema. The rich, dramatic and somber voice-over of Paul Frees gives us a quick, pre-credits lesson in meteorites and the unknown properties which many of them contain, as we witness a particular-

US poster (art by Reynold Brown)

ly large specimen plummet to ground on the outskirts of town, scattering hundreds of black fragments across the surrounding desert landscape. As a Federal geologist and a preteen schoolgirl soon discover in separate incidents, these unearthly pieces of rock contain a very strange atomic makeup, likely exacerbated by eons spent hotrodding around the galaxy, and the intense heat generated by Earth's atmospheric friction. Much like the titular creatures in Joe Dante's **GREMLINS** (1984, USA), exposure to normal H_2O causes these meteor fragments to do some pretty cool but rather terrifying things, as the water makes the rocks grow rapidly into black, crystal-like stalagmites. Once these monoliths grow to a humongous size, they topple over from their weight, not only crushing anything that happens to be in their way, but breaking-up into hundreds of smaller shards, each one of which proceeds to grow into a full-grown monolith of its own, thus repeating the cycle exponentially.

Though the local doctor, newspaperman and police chief are stumped, it doesn't take long for Dave Miller (Grant Williams), head of the local district geological office, and his old college professor, Arthur Flanders (Trevor Bardette) to suspect that the mysterious rock fragments found out in the desert are somehow connected with the strange events that are starting to occur in town.

Apart from flattening anything they happen to collapse upon, the meteor fragments also drains and absorbs silicon from everything they touch, from the desert sand to pet dogs and human beings, causing those exposed to it for too long to be turned into a solid, stone-like mass (much like the victims of the infamous, mythical gorgon). Naturally, the Main Street of San Angelo is directly in the irrevocable path of the multiplying monoliths, and a torrential downpour triggers a growth spurt that guarantees the destruction of the whole town, and—once the monoliths make it out of the desert valley—potentially the whole world besides.

With time running precariously short, Miller and Flanders have mere hours to try and unlock the mysteries of the alien rock, and concoct a formula to combat it. Will they succeed? Well, this is a 1950s Universal genre flick, so no prizes for guessing that the town and most of the main characters in it survive; the solution to the advancing enemy being found in the combination of a dry salt lake bed and a huge nearby irrigation dam built to water surrounding citrus farms.

One of the truly great aspects of **THE MONO-LITH MONSTERS** is that it doesn't feature any "true" monsters as such, yet its inanimate, towering villains are much more terrifying than most rubber-suited creatures of the day, because the

That ominous rumbling in the distance can only mean one thing...
THE MONOLITH MONSTERS are coming!

Teetering Towers Of Terror! A US lobbycard for one of the more offbeat alien invasion films of the 1950s

film's strange science seems almost plausible, and there's something unsettling in the way the monoliths duplicate and spread almost like a malignant tumor, running rampant. They don't seem intrinsically *evil*, they are just doing what they do when their strange chemistry mixes with ours. And this makes them even more imposing and unsettling, as they are beyond any kind of reasoning or sudden change of mind or direction.

Considering its budget, the special effects in **THE MONOLITH MONSTERS** are remarkably well-realized and impressive. There's a combination of miniatures, matte paintings and superimpositions that really suit the atmosphere and tone of the film, even the sequence with the small chunk of crystal suddenly growing in the laboratory sink, before smashing to pieces against the rim, looks remarkable. The effects keep you in the film, but also make you smile and nod approvingly at the skill on display, achieved with just a few basic materials and not much money, but plenty of ingenuity, imagination and artistry.

Like most of the other Universal monster and sci-fi classics from this period, the black & white cinematography (by Ellis W. Carter) really helps lend an atmosphere of menace and mystery to the film, and there's a terrific, taut score composed by Henry Mancini, Irving Getz and Herman Stein. Sound

effects are also very important in this film, as they add much dramatic weight to certain shots, such as the oncoming storm ominously brewing through the deserted nighttime streets of San Angelo, and the loud cracking sounds which the monoliths make as they grow and topple.

As he did so well in **THE INCREDIBLE SHRINKING MAN**, Grant Williams turns in a fine lead performance as Dave Miller. Like his Scott Carey in **SHRINKING MAN**, Miller is handsome, charismatic and strong, but has a slight off-center quality about him which makes him so interesting and enjoyable to watch. It's a pity he didn't do more genre films at the time (by 1972, he had reached the Al Adamson stage of his career, appearing in Al's no-budget wonder **BRAIN OF BLOOD**). Grant gets good support here from Lola Albright as Cathy, Miller's requisite love interest and the local grade school teacher, and especially from Les Tremayne as Martin Cochrane, the jaded local newspaperman wondering what he's still doing hanging around San Angelo, where "the big story" is never likely to happen. Tremayne excelled at these types of roles, and his performance here is up there with those in George Pal/Byron Haskin's **THE WAR OF THE WORLDS** (1953), Sid Pink/Ib Melchior's **THE ANGRY RED PLANET** (1959 [see *Monster!* #3, p.10]) and Jack Kevan/Irvin Berwick's **THE**

MONSTER OF PIEDRAS BLANCAS (1959 [see *Monster!* #2, p.3 & #5, p.4], all USA). Familiar face and fan fave William Schallert also turns in a fun little cameo appearance in the present film as a weather bureau man.

John Sherwood worked primarily as a second unit director or AD, particularly on a lot of 1950s westerns. He only has three feature films to his credit as main director: **THE MONOLITH MONSTERS, THE CREATURE WALKS AMONG US** (1956, USA) and the '56 Western **RAW EDGE**, with Rory Calhoun, Mara Corday, Yvonne De Carlo, Rex Reason and Neville Brand. On the strength of his two genre films (I love the somewhat offbeat **CREATURE WALKS!**), I am keen to see what he brought to the Western table. Unfortunately, **RAW EDGE** does not seem to be commercially available at the moment, other than on the grey-area collector's market. *[There is an English-language US trailer for said oater on YouTube at the French link "1956 - Raw Edge - La Proie des Hommes", but that seems to be the only video upload pertaining to the film at the site. Ad-copy from said trailer goes: "The Wild Oregon Frontier Where Violent Men Made Their Own Law And Every Woman Lived On The RAW EDGE Of Jeopardy... With Bullet-Blasting Fury He Challenged A Lawless Empire" –ed.]*

Who knows what other treats Sherwood might have given us if he hadn't died at the young age of 56, only two years after **THE MONOLITH MONSTERS** was released. But what little he did give monster movie fans were terrific contributions to what was a heavily-saturated genre at the time.

SUBURBAN GOTHIC

Reviewed by Steven Ronquillo

USA, 2014. D: Richard Bates, Jr.

The ghost comedy has been a staple since the silent days of cinema, and when done right is always worth some shivers and giggles. From George Marshall's **THE GHOST BREAKERS** (1940, USA) to Ivan Reitman's **GHOSTBUSTERS** (1984, USA), we have loved them—and loved being spooked by them—through the years. So, what did Richard Bates, Jr. decide to do as a follow-up to his beloved movie **EXCISION** (2012, USA), and does he fall prey to the dangers of the sophomore slump, or does he knock it out of the park? Let's find out, shall we...

Raymond (Matthew Gray Gubler) is a college graduate who, because he can't get a job, has to move back to live at home with his parents: His mother Eve (Barbara Niven) is carrying on an unsubtle flirtation with the head of the remodeling crew who are redoing their back yard, and his father Donald (Ray Wise) is the blueprint/poster boy for the middle-aged asshole jock douchebag racist (sample dialogue exchange between father and son: "Son, do you speak Mexican?" – "No, Dad, no one speaks 'Mexican'. They speak *Spanish*." – "I don't care. They're from Mexico. So they speak Mexican; only folks from Spain speak Spanish!") Along with meeting Becca (Kat Dennings), the local neighborhood bartender/badass with a crowbar, the workers dig up a coffin with a little girl's body inside…and then the ghostly mayhem starts, with Raymond discovering his long-lost ability to not just see ghosts but also to actually communicate with them. From there it blends together the horrible relationship between he and his father and the ghostly hijinks.

I love how every little thing in this movie pays off, from Raymond's pills to the sad story of the ghosts. One of my biggest gripes about ghost comedies is typically their lack of balance: they are either wacky as in "ha-ha", or neither sufficiently wacky nor scary enough. This one keeps the boos and ha-ha's well-balanced, and I like that. The scares themselves always have that creepy edge which helps maintain harmony between the giggles and the shivers. Such as in the scene wherein a teenage Raymond sees a ghost stripping for

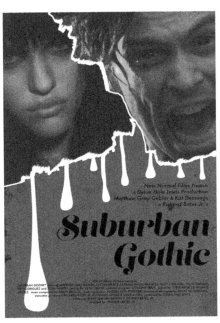

him and she gives him her tongue, or when Becca starts vomiting eyeballs after being cursed by a ghost, or—my personal fave—when the a-hole dickweed dad gets his just desserts.

Performance-wise, everyone does amazingly well, with Ray Wise stealing the movie every time he opens his big racist mouth and sticks his foot in it. Appealing young leads Gruber and Dennings display great chemistry and comic timing as Becca and Raymond, and there is some amazing work done elsewhere too, including the hilarious cameo put in by Jeffrey Combs as the doctor who has been treating Raymond his entire life; as well as welcome appearances by John Waters and Sally Kirkland as workers at the local historical society. These scenes add a lot of extra spice to the mix and make this highly enjoyable romp that much more special. The movie also contains my favorite line of dialogue from any movie released last year, but I don't think I ought to quote it in *Monster!* because this is an "R"-rated comedy all the way, so there's profanity involved (then again, I can't resist quoting it, so I will: "I'm a fucking wizard sent back from the future to tell you how worthless you fucking are!").

It's nice to see a spook comedy geared to adults, without them dumbing it down for a younger audience. Containing more gags than can be properly absorbed in just a single viewing, **SUBURBAN GOTHIC** ends with an amazing last shot that has the promise of so many ways in which it could be followed-up. It also has a fine-fun soundtrack that had me wanting to find a copy, to boot! Unfortunately, this is a movie which in this day and age is in danger of getting lost in the shuffle. Because, sadly, not even ten years ago a movie like this would have gotten a much wider release, but now movies like this have become merely disposable flavor-of-the-week VOD releases, and are just as easily forgotten by the following week. This is the kind of fun movie you can watch over and over again and not get tired of, however. As of this writing the film is on Amazon VOD, and it's worth every penny it takes to rent it. Because, if we don't show our love for them with our cash, amazing movies like this simply will not get produced.

So, a big "Bravo!" goes out to Richard Bates, Jr. for not falling victim to the dreaded sophomore slump, and likewise to his awesome cast for making one of the most fun ghost movies ever, so... *sequel, pleaze!* I promise I'll even clean my room and take the dog out for walkies if you make it.

Above: Kat Dennings displays her exceptional hand/eye coordination in **SUBURBAN GOTHIC. Top:** A spooky apparition from the same film

PARASITE

Reviewed by Michael Elvidge

USA, 1982. D: Charles Band

Ad-line: *"Once it gets inside you, it will do anything to get out!"*

PARASITE was a 3-D motion picture released on March 12 of '82 by Embassy Pictures, and theatergoers really got to experience the full effect of this feature as billed: *"The First Futuristic Monster Movie In 3-D!"* The only other horror film in the same format out at that time was Steve Miner's slasher **FRIDAY THE 13TH PART 3**. When I was a kid in the 1980s, during the VHS home video era, I missed the present film on its theatrical run, but the box art really stood out, and I eventually rented the film on tape. Years later when I picked up the Anchor Bay edition of **PARASITE** on DVD, the artwork had now changed from the toothy critter with "3-D" expanding out of its mouth to a photo of Demi Moore in there instead...but we'll get to that later.

Set in the future world of 1992 (!), after a limited nuclear war, scientist Dr. Paul Dean (Robert Glaudini) works in a laboratory for the new government, run by "The Merchants". The film opens with the doctor strapped onto a bed as smoke and eerie red lighting ominously set the stage for his ensuing nightmare. While developing a new biological weapon—the titular otherwise nameless parasitical organism—he accidentally infects himself with one of the creatures during a scuffle with a Merchant. Paul takes another parasite in a canister with him when he escapes from the Merchants, who wear dark suits and white shirts and have an "X" logo tattooed on the backs of their hands signifying their allegiance to the all-powerful Xyrex Corporation, a company that took over after the collapse of the American government. The good doctor makes his getaway inside a stolen Xyrex ambulance and drives off, whereafter he reaches an apparently deserted out-in-the-middle-of-nowhere place called "Work Camp 34", which is fenced-in and crawling with snakes and tarantulas (well, *sort of*, as only one of each of those is shown). A woman's screams shortly lead Dr. Dean to investigate a nearby building, where he finds two thugs attacking the woman. Paul scares them off with a laser gun, and a slow-motion fight breaks out. Afterwards he releases the woman from the ropes they had bound her with only to find she was a willing participant in the whole "ordeal" (i.e., kinky scene). After this incident, the doctor is thanked by an older man named Buddy (James Cavan), who, sick of those lawless (quote) "Sickies", invites Paul into his place for a cup of coffee. Once inside, Paul begins to feel some of the ill effects of the parasitic infection; in a later scene, his infected abdomen looks like one of James Woods' stomach-opening hallucinations from David Cronenberg's **VIDEODROME** (1982, Canada). Paul shortly leaves Buddy's house and the thugs pull a surprise ambush on him, but during a struggle one of the attackers is bitten by a rattlesnake…right before Dr. Dean plunges a metal pipe into his stomach (making for an ideal "3-D" effect as the camera zooms in for a foreshortened C/U shot of the impaled man's blood pouring from the outer end of the pipe in the extreme foreground).

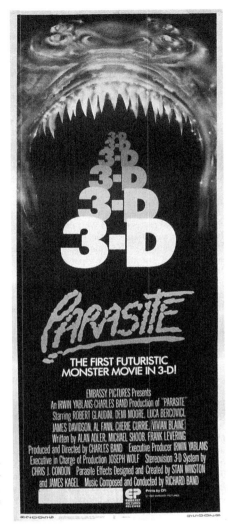

Dean thereafter hits the road again till he finds a small town called Joshua (population 64), where he sets up a makeshift lab in a hotel room he rents at the sarcastically-named "Joshua Hilton". A Merchant named Wolf (James Davidson, who is mostly known for playing bit-parts in '60s/'70s American TV shows; his part here was actually one of his largest, and he is highly convincing indeed in the role) is sent to find Dean, and arrives in a whirring black Lamborghini Countach; Wolf is also equipped with the meanest up-the-sleeve (laser) gun you've ever seen since Travis Bickle's similarly stashed concealed firearm in De Niro/Scorsese's **TAXI DRIVER** (1976, USA). At a rundown eatery called Collins' New York Bar, Grill & Barter, Paul barters his wristwatch for some soup,

and after still more local thugs enter and begin to hassle him, we are introduced to the local hottie, lemon-grower Patricia Welles (future "superstar" Demi Moore). Dean has a run-in with the gang, whereupon they steal the canister with the parasite inside from the scientist's room. Ignoring his warnings not to open the container, gang member Zeke foolishly pops the lid open and the lurking parasite lunges out and attaches its corrosively toxic body to his chest.

Now the *real* fun begins...

Wolf enters the first town Paul encountered and talks with Buddy about Paul's whereabouts. Buddy plays stupid and claims he knows nothing. A blast from Wolf's quick-draw zapper punitively severs Buddy's hand ("I really *hate* liars!"). Traveling on to Joshua, Wolf goes to the NYBG&B and orders a glass of Patricia's refreshing homemade lemonade, then plugs for info about Paul from Collins a.k.a. "Scarface" (well-played by the prolific African-American character actor Al Fann, from William Friedkin's **THE FRENCH CONNECTION** [1971, USA] *et al*). Paul's stolen ambulance is found hidden under tarps behind Joshua's Xyrex service station by Wolf; the mouthy gas attendant, armed with a gun, lies that he hasn't seen anyone, however. The room Paul has taken at the so-called Joshua Hilton is also discovered by Wolf, and, when Paul returns to retrieve his equipment with Patricia, Wolf watches from concealment and then follows them. While in pursuit, Ricus' gang grab Wolf but his sneaky hidden laser slices off one of the gang members' ears, and Wolf then escapes in his car. Back at Patricia's house, Paul explains how the parasite is now in a dormant stage, but when it matures will cast millions of spores into the air. Wherever a spore touches anyone, a parasite will grow... To cut a lo-o-ong story short, a high-frequency sonic device turned up full-throttle causes the parasite infecting Paul to split its way out of his stomach, leading into the exciting, pyrotechnics-filled climax.

To focus on the actual monster in the film, the parasite, it makes several appearances and evolves into a larger version towards the end of the film; very leech-like and resembling a worm/tadpole hybrid, with an enormous mouth full of pointed teeth. Gooey and goopy, the parasite leaves snail-style gunk trails when slithering about. With the power to leap in a split-second, attaching itself to its victims, this makes the parasite a formidably monstrous opponent indeed. Trying to remove the parasite once it latches on lamprey-like is hopeless, as, able to secrete a corrosive substance, it can burrow into the vic-

tim's body and eventually burst out when it's consumed its fill of the unwilling host organism. Some of these bursting scenes inevitably bring to mind Ridley Scott's **ALIEN** (1979, USA/UK). In a leg-chomping moment we see that the parasite is capable of sinking its formidable array of pointy teeth into large chunks of human flesh. The second parasite spends most of the film's duration incubating patiently inside Dr. Dean's stomach. As a bonus, the makeup effects were designed by Stan Winston and James Kagel. Winston of course went on to win the Academy Award and later worked on monster blockbusters like James Cameron's **ALIENS** (1986, USA) and Steven Spielberg's **JURASSIC PARK** (1993, USA).

Actress Demi Moore here received her first film role as a lead with the character Patricia Wells. Shortly after **PARASITE**, Moore's career stepped into an A-list phase. As mentioned above, the DVD releases of **PARASITE** prominently feature Moore on the cover, because she had long been a mega-celeb by then. Main character Paul Dean, Robert Glaudini, besides being an actor is also a playwright, director and drama teacher. His filmography spans some 15 titles, including such diverse and disparate fare as **THE ALCHEMIST** (1981, USA) and **THE PRINCESS DIARIES** (2001, USA). Glaudini's off-Broadway play, *Jack Goes Boating*, starred the late Philip Seymour Hoffman among other notables, and a motion picture adaptation directed by Hoffman hit theaters in September 2010 (Robert's actress daughter Lola Glaudini filled a supporting role in it). Luca Bercovici, who played the not-entirely-despicable Ricus here, subsequently turned director, making his debut in that capacity on Empire Pictures' **GHOULIES** (1984, USA), another film on which the Band Bros. placed their brand; with Charles executive-producing and Richard composing its score. In **PARASITE**, the late Tom

Cherie Currie gets chomped in **PARASITE**

Villard (1953-1994) plays the character Zeke, one of Ricus' punky gang. He may be best-known to horror fans from his role as Toby in Mark Herrier's and Alan Ormsby's horror spoof **POPCORN** (1991, USA). Another thug gang member of note herein is Dana, played by Cherie Currie (the lead singer of the all-girl rock group The Runaways, who are arguably best-known for the raucous rocker "Cherry Bomb"); Currie's first film role was in Adrian Lyne's teen drama **FOXES** (1980), and she subsequently appeared in "It's a Good Life", the Joe Dante-directed third segment of the SF/horror anthology **TWILIGHT ZONE: THE MOVIE** (1983). She reunited with actor Glaudini on the sci-fi flick **WAVELENGTH** (1983, all USA). Another interesting career note related to horror films is that Currie did Automated Dialog Replacement (ADR)—more popularly known as "looping" voice tracks—on Manny Coto's horror comedy **DR. GIGGLES** (1992, USA/Japan), starring Larry Drake in the title role. Aging glamor girl Vivian Blaine (1921-1995) costars in **PARASITE** as a rooming-house owner (that fine establishment known as the Joshua Hilton), but she's best-known for her roles on Broadway.

When watching the 2-D version of the film, you can still see some of what would have stood out in the original 3-D process (the "pipe" scene described above, for example). There is the required odd camera work and use of lighting to create depth. The soundtrack is another key component of the film, and was composed by Richard Band, brother of Charles, the film's director (they are the sons of legendary producer Albert Band [1924-2002]). Richard scored many more film soundtracks afterwards, notably including Stuart Gordon's **RE-ANIMATOR** (1985) and **FROM BEYOND** (1986, both USA), as well as numerous TV scores too. Recently, Charles Band made a controversial decision to rerelease Wizard big-box VHS tapes of rare horror films in overpriced limited editions online, pinching the nerve of the diehard VHS collectors' community.

The budget of **PARASITE** was approximately $800,000, and the film grossed some $7,000,000 in the USA. A sequel was announced in 1983, but it didn't happen. An advertisement with the proposed-but-unrealized second film's poster art appeared in *Variety* magazine, accompanied by the following catchphrase which suggests that the plot's milieu was to be a high-rise building ("*27 Floors of Living, Creeping, Shocking 3-D... PARASITE 2: THE TERROR CONTINUES*"). If that was the case, the base premise seems similar to Cronenberg's **SHIVERS** (a.k.a. **THEY CAME FROM WITHIN**, 1975, Canada), which dealt with other parasites on the loose in an apartment complex. The **PARASITE** sequel's proposed production company Embassy Pictures went out of business and Band's new company Empire Pictures was set to produce the film, with star Glaudini due to reprise his role as Dr. Paul Dean. The original film gained a small if loyal cult following, and is often referenced by other filmmakers in their productions: a **PARASITE** poster is seen in the background in **TROLL** (1986, USA), and another sighting includes a VHS box with the film's title on view in Don Dohler's **BLOOD MASSACRE** (1991, USA). **PARASITE** was even put on the so-called "Video Nasties" list in the UK for a time.

Having not gotten a chance to see it when **PARASITE** originally opened theatrically (at eight years old in 1982, I was too young to attend a screening), I was eventually able to see some 3-D horror films in the theater, including Rachel Talalay's **FREDDY'S DEAD: THE FINAL NIGHTMARE** (1991, USA). In the 1980s I did catch a 3-D version of Julian Roffman's horror film **THE MASK** (a.k.a. **EYES OF HELL**, 1961, Canada) when it played on Canadian TV. Not the most popular of horror films, **PARASITE** still provides sufficient slimy sustenance and makes for infectious entertainment nonetheless. With Charles Band's new ventures into big-box VHS and magazines lately, maybe we'll be lucky enough in the future to see a release of a 3-D version of the film in order to better enjoy all the *"Creeping, Shocking Terror!"*

FINAL THOUGHTS

75

Louis Paul's
CREATURE FEATURES
HAMMER REDUX

I have written about a number of movies released by the British studio, Hammer Films in previous issues of Monster! *As well, other writers have chimed in with their opinions and reviews with their own observations in these pages, so I don't wish to be redundant and go over the history of the studio again, since I've tackled that in the past in this 'zine.*

I believe it's time to cover some of the less popular titles (for example, last issue Troy Howarth wrote about their Dracula *series of films, and I covered Hammer's* Frankenstein *films). While the titles covered in this article are far from what could be classified as obscure, they do receive less mention nowadays than in previous years, so they have become somewhat lesser-known. Worthy titles to be discussed for a variety of reasons, they also document, in their own way, Hammer's efforts to present movies outside the sphere of their most popular releases of the time.*

There are a few other titles that are also noteworthy of mention, but I believe they've also been documented in previous issues of M!—and if not...I might write about those in future instalments of this column.

But for now, feast your eyes on Hammer's attempts to bring to the world of the 'Sixties and 'Seventies...zombies, humanoid snake monsters, bodice-popping vampire twins plus even more unusual vampires; and, finally, their own take on satanic cults and exorcisms (which albeit came a couple years too late to cash in on **THE EXORCIST**).

THE PLAGUE OF THE ZOMBIES
UK, 1965. D: John Gilling
Wr: Anthony Nelson Keys
S: André Morell, John Carson, Jacqueline Pearce, Diane Clare, Brook Williams

This movie takes place in Cornwall, England (but its exteriors were actually shot in Black Park, Buckinghamshire, where most of the studio's outdoor scenes were filmed). The time period is the mid-1800s, and the inhabitants of a small village are besieged by an unexplainable plague which appears to be taking a major toll on the inhabitants. Local doctor Thompson (Williams) seeks aid from his old scholastic friend, a fellow former adventurer named Sir James Forbes (Morell).

Not sure what to make of this virus or plague that causes its victims to become pasty-faced living dead people, when they open the coffins of the most-recent victims, they find them...empty. An inexplicable turn of events, for sure. The wooden boxes are empty because locals are now spot-

In **PLAGUE**, John Carson as the villainous squire and one of his flunkies perform a zombie-making ritual involving a Voodoo doll

ting the walking dead out in the local marshland, within the vicinity of an old mine. It doesn't take Sir James (a Van Helsing stand-in) long to figure out that the decidedly arrogant and corrupt Squire

Hamilton (Carson) may have something to do with all this. When Sir James discovers that the Squire was in Haiti for a number of years, and witnessed voodoo rituals firsthand, his suspicions grow. What the squirrely Squire is up to and why he is so compelled to create a mini army of the undead is best left to discovery by the viewer, so I don't really want to spoil it all by recounting the entire film, scene by scene. But I will mention that once our villain sets his sights on Sir James' daughter, he will resort to using poison and hypnotism to try turning her into his love slave…and of course, those zombies are nearby; the reanimated dead with weathered rags for clothing.

Something of a rarity in the Hammer Film canon, this is one of the very few titles in their filmography to feature zombies. Two years before George Romero's **NIGHT OF THE LIVING DEAD** (1968, USA), **PLAGUE** gets little respect for even broaching the subject matter, albeit in quite a stylized and low-key manner as done here. André Morell leads the quite capable cast of pro actors (he was earlier seen in the BBC's *Quatermass and the Pit* serial [1958; see *Monster!* #11], and was

also memorable as Dr. Watson [alongside Peter Cushing as Holmes] in Hammer's **THE HOUND OF THE BASKERVILLES** [1959, UK]). The present film deals with such themes as conflict between the classes (the upper versus the lower), as well as working in such other thematic concerns as mysticism, repressed sexuality, and, of course, the occult. The zombies are slow-moving, chiefly male, and all clad in torn, aged shrouds (regardless of how long they have been dead and buried). Ashen, with mud caked on their faces and hands, rather than reach out and tear flesh, these zombies simply grab and throttle their victims.

The film's director, John Gilling, was a TV veteran who also directed two of Hammer's swashbuckling pirate adventures (**THE PIRATES OF BLOOD RIVER** [1962] and **THE CRIMSON BLADE** [1963]), the gothic thriller **THE SHADOW OF THE CAT** (1962, all UK), also starring Morell, and the terrific independent Brit sci-fi film **THE NIGHT CALLER** (a.k.a. **NIGHT OF THE BLOOD BEAST**, 1965) with John Saxon. He directed **PLAGUE** in '65 and **THE REPTILE** in '66, before doing one more Ham-

One of the freakier scenes from **THE PLAGUE OF THE ZOMBIES**

78

mer (**THE MUMMY'S SHROUD** in '67). In the same period he also helmed the Eurospy favorite **WHERE THE BULLETS FLY** (1966, UK), starring Tom Addams as suave, lecherous ladies' man Charles Vine.

Most of Gilling's output post these films in the late '60s and early '70s was dozens of episodes of British small screen genre favorites like *The Saint*, *The Champions*, and *Department S*. His last movie was **CROSS OF THE DEVIL** (*La cruz del diablo*, 1975, Spain), which was written by Paul Naschy, who later dismissed, disowned and derided the film. Rumor has it that while at his vacation home in Spain, Gilling was approached by Naschy to direct this horror film based on the work he did for Hammer in the '60s. Slow, and often impenetrable, the movie, based on the writings of Edgar Allan Poe, was about an opium-addicted writer who sees visions, and investigates the murder of his sister. The Knights Templar also figure into the story briefly…for years confusing people into thinking that this was the unofficial fifth entry to Amando de Ossorio's *Blind Dead* quadrilogy.

Jacqueline Pearce became a fan favorite for her appearances in her two hammer movies, but, aside from these, she worked almost exclusively for British television, with notable roles in *Dr. Who*, *Blake's 7*, and others.

Critically well-regarded for its deliberate pacing and atmosphere, **THE PLAGUE OF THE ZOMBIES** (see also *Monster!* #10) was one of Hammer's "let's try something different" titles in a period where they were mostly cranking out Dracula and Frankenstein movies.

THE REPTILE

UK, 1966. D: John Gilling
Wr: Anthony Nelson Keys
S: *Jacqueline Pearce, Noel Willman, Ray Barrett, Jennifer Daniel, Michael Ripper*

Also set in a village in Cornwall (just like the previous film), **THE REPTILE** (see also *Monster!* #10) tells a sort of similar tale. However, instead of a voodoo-like cult presided over by a madman who has resurrected the dead, this time another erudite crazy, Dr. Franklyn (Willman), who has returned from the Far East with his pretty, "teenaged" daughter (Pearce, who is obviously not a teenager) in tow, uses rituals and dark occult rites learned from his stay in India, and is responsible for a number of murders. Upon returning to his family home with his newlywed bride (Daniel) at his side, Harry (Barrett) learns that the formerly quiet village has become a fog-enshrouded dark

Italian poster for **THE REPTILE** (art unsigned)

place where the once-happy townsfolk have grown suspicious and resentful. Dr. Franklyn appears to have a bizarre relationship with his daughter (Pearce). Openly treating her with spite and scorn in front of the staff and others, he also treats her as a veritable slave, preventing her from conversing with others, and having friends.

One will not need a dissertation in psychosexual analysis to figure out that the same nights as this woman feels certain sexual urges, is when people die… In time, we discover that, due to some rather obliquely-referenced "thing" that happened to her while in India—maybe some sexual transgression was involved?—the daughter was cursed and, well…*changes* into a scaly, large-fanged reptilian monster when she gets pissed-off. Wisely (*sort of*), her dad keeps a manservant on call to attend to his daughter, this so as to prevent her from going completely snaky and biting everyone in sight.

Directed by John Gilling as part of a one-two punch of Hammer horrors in '66, the director—referenced by some of his coworkers from the period as being "temperamental"—worked with a good cast of British actors. Noel Willman, who was extremely effective as Dr. Ravna in Hammer's **KISS OF THE VAMPIRE** (a.k.a. **KISS OF EVIL**, 1963, UK), is here, as well as perennial Hammer "face" Michael Ripper as a bartender.

Like **PLAGUE**, a similar atmosphere of fog-drenched terror enveloping small-town England also permeates this horror film, which takes all kinds of twists and turns and even hints at some sexual themes not generally tackled in British terror films of the early-to-mid-'Sixties. Roy Ashton was responsible for Jacqueline Pearce's colorful and striking makeup when she turns into the humanoid reptile monster, and the ghastly gory post-bite marks were shocking for their time; not so much nowadays in retrospect, but still worthy of applause considering the time period in which the film was made. Sadly, along with **THE PLAGUE OF THE ZOMBIES**, what **THE REPTILE** lacks is a strong male lead actor and character. I got the strong impression, and maybe I'm not incorrect in saying this, but just possibly the director was more concerned with mood, setting, and themes than he was in making a strong impression with romanticism or heroic acts performed.

TWINS OF EVIL
UK, 1971. D: John Hough
Wr: Tudor Gates
S: Peter Cushing, Mary & Madeline Collinson, Damien Price, David Warbeck, Katya Wyeth, Dennis Price, Luan Peters

As **TWINS** begins, we find ourselves in overcast and cold Karnstein…a familiar village to fans of Hammer's Frankenstein and Dracula lore, and for those who were pleased with the lesbian fang-and-breast-baring opus **THE VAMPIRE LOVERS** (1970, UK/USA), which is a prequel of sorts to this movie.

Voluptuous twin sisters Maria and Frieda (Mary and Mads Collinson) move from their-swinging early 1800s Vienna to live in Karnstein with their puritanical relatives, specifically the stoic and iron-willed General Gustav Weil (Cushing). Both girls become attracted to the sensual and magnetic Count Karnstein (Price), while also receiving the attentions of a young occult scholar named Anton (Warbeck). It doesn't take them long to discover that Uncle Gustav is a part-time witch-hunter who leads a gang of self-righteously pious and misguided menfolk known as "The Brotherhood". Gustav clearly dislikes the lecherous and wealthy Count, but since he is in favor with royalty he remains untouchable by the local authorities. Gustav comes to strongly suspect that Count Karnstein might be involved in Satanism and Black Magic—and, of course, he *is*—having been turned into a vampire by his deceased—and recently resurrected—relative, Countess Mircalla Karnstein (Wyeth), who enjoys his human sacrifice so much that she buries her fangs deep into the Count's neck.

When Frieda becomes a vampire due to indulging in a nocturnal tryst with the Count, her breasts appear to enlarge even more, and she blossoms… into a deadly vampire succubus! Fearing that "The Brotherhood" will enact a penalty of death on her sister, Maria tries to cover for Frieda, but is captured by the Count and his cronies in an attempt to exchange one sister for another when the "The Brotherhood" captures the latter twin on one of her nightly blood-seeking excursions, and she is trapped in a cell by them. Anton, who is now

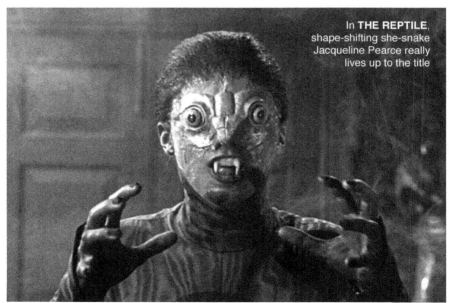

In **THE REPTILE**, shape-shifting she-snake Jacqueline Pearce really lives up to the title

in love with Maria, learns that a switch has been made and rushes to prevent her death by being burned alive as he joins with her Uncle Gustav and they storm Castle Karnstein, where they have their final confrontation with both the Count and Frieda. One of the most notorious and lurid of all Hammer Film productions (obviously influenced by the financial successes of titles like Michael Reeves' **WITCHFINDER GENERAL** [1968, UK] and Michael Armstrong's and Adrian Hoven's **MARK OF THE DEVIL** [*Hexen bis aufs Blut gequält*, 1970, West Germany]), **TWINS OF EVIL** is jam-packed with shape-shifting vampires and sex (etc). It was directed by John Hough, whose filmography, while not overly prolific at only 30 credits, contains a number of "WTF were they thinking?!" kind of movies like the equally lurid, crazed "boy who cried wolf" assassination thriller **EYEWITNESS** (a.k.a. **SUDDEN TERROR**, 1970, UK); **THE LEGEND OF HELL HOUSE** (1973, UK)—a strange unofficial remake of **THE HAUNTING** (1963, UK/USA)—wherein Pam Franklin gets to have sex with an invisible ghost amidst a hysterical cast shouting and screaming at unseen demons; the cult classic fugitives-on-the-run madness that is **DIRTY MARY, CRAZY LARRY** (1974, USA); and the demonic rape shocker **THE INCUBUS** (1982, Canada), that latter featuring a very, *very* strange performance by star John Cassavetes. In between all those he helmed a couple of *Avengers* episodes (the Linda Thorson ones), and of course the western **TRIUMPHS OF A MAN CALLED HORSE** (1983, USA/Canada/Spain), where we got to see Richard Harris endure nearly unbearable tortures all over again.

Peter Cushing, usually a dependable stalwart force of reason (even if it is sometimes misguided, with a touch of insanity, as in the Hammer *Frankenstein* series [see *Monster!* #13]), delivers one of his more unusual (and unlikable) performances as Gustav, an intolerant man with no compassion and a driving obsession to rid the Earth of all evil, and using evil means to do it. "The young must be chastised!" he exclaims in one scene before beating one of the twins who has been covering up for her vampiric sibling.

David Warbeck went on to play heroic leading man in several Antonio Margheriti-directed adventure films of the '80s (including **THE ARK OF THE SUN GOD** [*I sopravvissuti della città morta*, 1984, Italy]), and was the doomed voice of reason in a few of Lucio Fulci's best (e.g. **THE BEYOND** [*...E tu vivrai nel terrore! L'aldilà*, 1981, Italy]). His performance in the present film is fine, but appearing in a movie opposite the distracting Collinson twins surely meant he would disappear into the background, and this is not one

French poster for **TWINS OF EVIL**
(art by Bacha)

of his more fleshed-out characters, making his performance appear indifferent to his surroundings.

Mary and Madeleine Collinson were identical twin sisters-turned-actresses, who appeared naked in at least one sexy short film directed by pioneering British softcore filmmaker Harrison Marks (namely *Halfway Inn* [1970, UK]). They can also be seen in such other sexploitation efforts as Lindsay Shonteff's **PERMISSIVE** and Derek Ford's **GROUPIE GIRL** (a.k.a. **I AM A GROUPIE**, both 1970, UK). A *Playboy* "Playmate of the Month" pictorial (the first ever to feature twins!) garnered them still more attention, whereafter they screen-tested and got the roles in **TWINS OF EVIL**. More recently, Mary was scheduled to appear (for the first time at a convention anywhere in the US) at the October 2011 Chiller Theatre con in New Jersey, but had to cancel. Madeleine died last August at the age of 62.

VAMPIRE CIRCUS
UK, 1972. D: Robert Young
Wr: Judson Kinberg
S: *Adrienne Corri, Robert Tayman, Laurence Payne, Thorley Walters, Lynne Frederick, John Moulder-Brown, Anthony Corlan, David Prowse*

One of Hammer's eeriest films begins with a prologue that sets up everything that is to follow. In the Austrian town of Shtetl, a schoolmaster witnesses his wife lure their young daughter to a castle, home of the reclusive Count Mitterhaus (Tay-

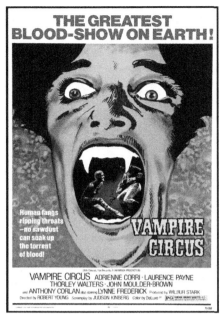

US one-sheet poster (art unsigned)

man), actually a vampire who with his servants has been thriving on the blood of young victims. When men from the town storm the castle and thrust a wooden stake through Mitterhaus' heart, he curses the villagers and all their descendants, vowing a blood oath that involves their children.

Nearly two decades later, Shtetl is besieged by a plague and the town has been cut off from surrounding villages, with the authorities placing a shoot-on-sight order for anyone caught trying to leave the area, so as to contain the plague. One of the few people allowed to enter Shtetl from the outside world is Dr. Kersh (Owens) who disbelieves the incredible stories about Castle Mitterhaus and vampirism, blaming it on simple superstition and myth…but the villagers know otherwise!

A traveling troupe of entertainers calling themselves the "Circus of the Night" shortly enters the town during the night, and they are welcomed by the villagers as a means to escape the harsh reality of being trapped inside an invisible hell while facing exposure to a plague from within, and with gun-toting soldiers surrounding the town on all sides to prevent their escape. This circus is beyond strange, as it only appears during the night, and is seemingly be run by a nutty gypsy woman (Corri) and her assistant, a dwarf clown (played by little person actor Skip Martin, previously seen as Vincent Price's court fool Hop Toad in Roger Cor-

man's **THE MASQUE OF THE RED DEATH** [1964, USA/UK] and subsequently as Michael Gough's half-pint henchman in Antony Balch's **HORROR HOSPITAL** [1973, UK]). The circus entertainment consists of Serena, a shapely, mostly nude woman with her entire body painted as if she was a tiger, and her "trainer" Milovan, who engage in a little erotic play as part of their act, a mute strongman (Prowse) who might well be deadlier than he seems, and the bizarre, handsome Emil (Corlan) who attracts the attention of the town's young women. Emil turns out to be a cousin of Count Mitterhaus, and is a shape-shifter and vampire as well. Emil and the gypsy enter Castle Mitterhaus in the dead of night, and, over his surprisingly well-preserved body, they reveal their plan to revive the Count by decimating all of Shtetl. With Dr. Kersh out of the picture (he snuck out to seek help from the government), it's up his son, Anton (Moulder-Brown), who is in love with Dora (Frederick) two young, full-blooded bodies ripe to be picked by the supernatural circus troupe for use in the resurrection of Count Mitterhaus.

The director Robert Young was an unusual choice to helm this movie, having been primarily a documentary filmmaker at the time. He worked mostly in television afterwards, with only one fairly notable credit in the mid-'70s, the sex farce **KEEP IT UP DOWNSTAIRS** (1976, UK), starring Jack Wild and Diana Dors; which was a bawdy spoof of the popular English period telly drama *Upstairs, Downstairs*. He also worked on some relatively obscure Britcoms for television too, and, in later years, he codirected (with Fred Schepisi) **FIERCE CREATURES** (1997, UK/USA), a failed belated attempt to repeat the success of the cult comedy hit, **A FISH CALLED WANDA** (1988, USA/UK) by reuniting that movie's main cast, including John Cleese and Jamie Lee Curtis.

In **TWINS**, the characters of Count Mitterhaus and his minions, and the village children corrupted by the circus, also bring up a very disturbing psychosexual subtext to the whole movie. Sewn into the celluloid dress of an erotic vampire horror melodrama, the film actually deals with the corruption by spiritual and physical lures, even touching ever-so-briefly on pedophilia.

Oddly enough, research I have done shows that some actual historical horror may have influenced some of the themes in the film, and possibly why Young was selected for the directing gig, since he had experience working on documentaries. Someone at Hammer knew his or her history, and thematically I believe events in the film echo and were influenced by deeds committed by the French nobleman and knight Gilles de Rais, once a companion of Joan of Arc. In 1434, de Rais retired from military service, and was held responsible for the deaths of hundreds of children murdered in his castle. Historical documents reported everything from rape, bloodletting, communal drinking of blood, to even cannibalism being committed. He was executed in 1440.

As the years have passed, **VAMPIRE CIRCUS** has gained much notoriety for its depiction of sexuality, as well as touching on some taboo subjects, such as the ones I've described above. However, in the end, as much as someone involved with the production liked to have thought they were being clever with the script, most of the leading characters are underwritten (possibly borne out by the fact that some of them don't even have any actual names), leading us to care little about their fate. And ultimately, the film pointed the direction in which Hammer would be heading: more sex, more horror, for better or worse.

TO THE DEVIL A DAUGHTER
UK/West Germany, 1976. D: Peter Sykes
Wr: Chris Wicking, John Peacock, Gerald Vaughan-Hughes; based on the novel by Dennis Wheatley
S: *Richard Widmark, Christopher Lee, Honor Blackman, Denholm Elliott, Nastassja Kinski*

American journalist and self-styled expert on the occult John Verney (Widmark) gets stuck with a barely post-pubescent girl named Catherine (Kinski) whom his good friend (Elliott) asked him to pick up from an airport in London. It turns out that she is a young nun living with "The Children of the Lord", actually a quasi-religious order that is based in Germany. The only time Catherine is permitted to leave the premises is to visit her father once a year. However, when Verney meets Catherine, for someone so young, she is strangely alluring, and quite mysterious. Verney learns that Catherine needs to be protected because she is in grave danger. Approaching her eighteenth birthday (Kinski was actually only fourteen when the movie was made, and she participated in a number of then-controversial nude scenes), Catherine is to be wedded and then sacrificed to Astaroth. With the combined forces of Satan and other dark powers, the cult wishes to unleash the Antichrist upon the world. In order to find the perfect child, the residents of the nunnery, led by excommunicated heretical nutcase priest Father Rayner (Lee) have murdered a number of women during childbirth, and those who escaped the ritualistic killings have also been tracked down and killed. Rayner will go to any lengths to retrieve Catherine and kill Verney.

Shocking in a way that very few Hammer films had been before it, **TO THE DEVIL A DAUGHTER** also manages to tarnish the grand legacy of horror that the studio had been responsible for in

the past by producing a movie influenced by William Friedkin's **THE EXORCIST** (1973, USA), Italian shock cinema (e.g., Alberto de Martino's depraved **THE ANTICHRIST** [*L'anticristo*, a.k.a. **THE TEMPTER**, 1974]), and dozens of lurid low-budget independent movies made in the USA. Director Peter Sykes worked as a documentarian and experimental filmmaker, and made a rock concert film in '68. After helming two of the worst episodes of the Linda Thorson-era *Avengers* in '69, he directed the bizarre British sexy shocker **VENOM** (a.k.a. **THE LEGEND OF SPIDER FOREST**, 1971, UK)—written and produced by sexploitation filmmaker Derek Ford—about a sadistic killer, a photographer who is an amateur detective and a whole lot of other nonsense besides. Afterward he made **DEMONS OF THE MIND** (1972, UK), one of the strangest Hammer Films; this one dealing with such topics as incest, hypnotism and psychokinesis. I would say it was most likely his work on that movie which got him the gig on **TO THE DEVIL...**, but after the present movie, besides a few jobs directing minor British television comedies, he spent years working on a movie about the son of God, called **JESUS** (a.k.a. **THE JESUS FILM**, 1979, USA), which was poorly received both critically and commercially. He died in 2006 at age 66.

Richard Widmark was a movie star! Coming to stardom in the 'Forties (his breakout film being Henry Hathaway's gritty *noir* classic **KISS OF DEATH** [1947, USA], in which he unforgettably played a psycho gangster named Tommy

Kinski publicity pose for **TO THE DEVIL A DAUGHTER**

83

You don't wanna know what's about to happen in this scene from **TO THE DEVIL A DAUGHTER**...then again, maybe you do. If so, watch the movie and find out!

Udo), his career took his earthy tough guy persona through a variety of crime films, westerns, and more. Widmark worked with just about every major Hollywood director. In '68 he played the title detective of Don Siegel's downbeat melodrama **MADIGAN**, whose character even expired at the finale, yet he was back playing the same character on the short-lived TV series of the same name in 1972-73. Around the time he starred in **TO THE DEVIL...** he was also seen in Stanley Kramer's **THE DOMINO PRINCIPLE,** with Gene Hackman, and Robert Aldrich's **TWILIGHT'S LAST GLEAMING**, with Burt Lancaster, so Widmark was no stranger to working with great directors, even those towards the end of their career or life. Maybe he didn't get along well with Sykes, but Widmark appears strangely disengaged throughout the present movie, and only briefly when interacting with Kinski does he show glimpses that he's not merely waiting for the lunch break. Turning in the type of non-committed performance that he so often did during this period (**STARSHIP INVASIONS**, anyone?), Chris Lee appears like he's biting his lower lip though most of his scenes, the best of which are filled with wide-eyed histrionics...maybe he just felt he owed Hammer one more movie? Lee's short-lived production company, Charlemagne, purchased the rights to a number of (British author) Dennis Wheatley's stories about the occult (a given since one of his best roles was in **THE DEVIL RIDES OUT** for Hammer in '67, itself adapted from a Wheatley novel). In 1973, his company independently financed the occult thriller **NOTHING BUT THE NIGHT** (from a book by author John Blackburn), wherein Lee starred as a high-ranking investigator. Met with mediocre box-office and

reviews, Lee appeared determined to film another Wheatley story, and was active in the production of **TO THE DEVIL A DAUGHTER**.

In hindsight, the film is remembered mostly for the (at the time considered shocking and controversial) nude scenes from the then only 14-year-old Natassaja Kinski, and for an approach to horror that felt far removed from what we were used to getting from Hammer Films of the past: for instance, mothers being tortured during childbirth, babies being murdered, and things become still more lurid and sick when Kinski is assaulted by a bloody demon on an altar. Whatever artistic recollections voiced by the surviving cast and crew in the documentary that appears on the Anchor Bay DVD release of the film can be laughably overlooked when one takes into account some of the low points in Hammer history reached by this movie.

Most prominently, the ending of **TO THE DEVIL A DAUGHTER** received a lot of attention... and derision. Cineastes often recall the energetic feats that Peter Cushing's Dr. Van Helsing character performed during the climax of Hammer's **DRACULA** (1958, UK [see *Monster!* #13])—when he agilely jumped onto and ran down a long tabletop, then leapt into the air and tore down some heavy window drapes, thus letting in deadly sunlight that puts paid to Dracula (Lee)—as one of the finest heroic climaxes in all of horror cinema. Shame that for Hammer's next-to-last movie (their final production **THE LADY VANISHES** in '79 was a complete failure, and nearly bankrupted the studio forcing them into hibernation for what seemed like decades), all our hero Richard Widmark does is bop the villainous satanic priest on the head with a rock...*roll credits!*

THE HOUSE OF RAMSAY

PART NINE

by Tim Paxton

Dramatic lobby card for Kiran Ramsay's **AAKHRI CHEEKH**, a Bollywood horror film influenced in part by Wes Craven's 1989 film **SHOCKER**

It's sad to say, but the era of Indian monster movies is pretty much over. There was a time when hulking monstrosities like those that inhabited the Ramsays' films were almost commonplace. Nowadays, most of the horror films from that country concern themselves with ghostly possession. In this instalment of "The House of Ramsay", we take a look at two of their lesser-known creature features:

3D SAAMRI
(a.k.a. ३डी सामरी, SAAMRI; SATAN)
India, 1985. D: Tulsi & Shyam Ramsay

The heyday of Ramsay horror seemed to be the mid-/late'80s, when they struck gold with a string of boffo box office hits. It began with **PURANA MANDIR** (1984 [see *Monster!* #4, p.9]), and went on to include **VEERANA** (1985), **TAHKHANA**, (1986 [see *M!* #3, p.53]), and **PURANI HAVELI** (1989). At least, those are the ones that most people remember when they wax nostalgic on Bollywood monster flicks. There are a few forgotten films, which include the mad mummy movie **DAK BANGLA** (1986 [see *M!* #2, p.39])

and **3D SAAMRI**. That latter, our present title under review, was the follow-up—albeit in character-name only—to **PURANA MANDIR** (although, according to the IMDb, an alternate Hindi title for **3D SAAMRI** was **PURANA MANDIR 2: SAAMRI**, so evidently someone may have been hoping to turn it into a franchise). Once seen it becomes easily understood why this film has generally been disregarded: there is little in it of note other than some unusual set designs, nice cinematography and its grungy-looking, yucky-faced zombie monster. Despite its shortcomings and the unfortunate fact that, as the title suggests, this film was also made to cash in on the only minimally popular 3D craze of the 1980s (which here in the West mostly happened from 1982 to '83),

Although the title on this VCD sleeve reflects the film's original stereoscopic format, the video sourced for this release is from a crappy VHS tape complete with mis-tracking and drop-outs. Hence, no 3D here!

3D SAAMRI does have the distinction of being one of the earliest such Indian productions (it was made one year after India's first 3D film, the Malayalam-language ghostly family comedy **MY DEAR KUTTICHATHAN** [D: Jijo Punnoose], which was a huge hit). **3D SAAMRI** was also released same year as the 3D superhero/masked avenger film **SHIVA KA INSAAF** (D: Raj N. Sippy) and the lyrically beautiful Malayalam-language fantasy film **POURNAMI RAAVIL** directed by A. Vincent.

I had hopes of finding a copy of **3D SAAMRI** in its original 3D form, but that wasn't in the cards. Neither the horrid quality VCD (sourced from a mistracking VHS tape) nor the DVD reissues bothered to produce remastered editions of the film. Now would be the time for the Ramsays

to dust off their master print of the film and re-issue it, as the market for 3D DVDs in India is incredibly lucrative at the moment. I have purchased five recent films on DVD that came with the required pair of green-and-blue glasses. To my displeasure, none of them work very well (and I have an HD TV and Blu-ray player, plus sit at the correct angle to view them, etc.), but that doesn't stop Indian distributors from releasing many stereoscopic "special editions", regardless. As with the rest of the world, India has their boatload of 3D movies made to capitalize on the popularity of this still-ongoing gimmick (because I hold that it is just that: a gimmick). And it seems that the most popular genre is the one which will usually—well, *hopefully*—make you jump the most when various objects are tossed at you from off the screen: *HORROR!* Recent films from this genre that I have seen include Vikram Bhatt's **CREATURE 3D** (2014 [see *M!* #10, p.11]) and the same director's **HAUNTED 3D** (2011), **DRACULA 2012** (2013, D: Vinayan), **BHOOT RETURNS** (2012, D: Ram Gopal Varma), **ZAPATLELA 2** (2013, D: Mahesh Kothare), and **RAKTHARAKSHASSU** (2014, D: Rupesh Paul). If the Ramsays had any sense, they would reissue **3D SAAMRI** in some kind of 30th Anniversary special edition DVD of the film. I've seen an excellent print of it online with English subtitles[1], so all of the elements are there for them to package the film for maybe a parallel rerelease with their (*shudder!*) new version of an old classic, **VEERANA 3D**, due out later this year. That would be a fun marketing tool when **V3D** hits the home video market: a "2in1" title, something which is not that uncommon with other newer Indian DVD releases. It won't happen, though, as the Ramsays don't seem too interested

---

1   Granted it was matted so as to appear widescreen, although the film itself was presumably originally lensed at the aspect ratio of 1.33:1, the standard "full-frame" which, until relatively recently, was how most of Bollywood shot their films. Although, that said and for what it's worth, the IMDb says that **3D SAAMRI**'s original theatrical aspect ratio was 2.35:1, so who knows?

The film's title card

in their older product, no matter how superior it is to the newer material they insist on churning out seemingly by rote while continually resting on their laurels and trying to capitalize on their past glories.

So, what's up with **3D SAAMRI**? In a way it *is* an in-name-only sequel to the above-cited earlier Ramsay monster movie called **PURANA MANDIR**, and, like that film, its plot does involve a vengeance-seeking monster called Saamri (sometimes also spelled Samri, less one "a"). In **PURANA MANDIR**, Saamri[2] was a hulking sorcerer (portrayed by the larger-than-life actor Anirudh Agarwal) who delighted in first draining the blood of, and then cannibalizing, local royalty. He is apprehended and sentenced to death, but—just before he has his head lopped-off—manages to toss out a curse at his captors, vowing to return from the dead to wreak his revenge at a later date. Saamri does indeed return, albeit a few hundred years down the pike, as a furry and fanged monstrosity. Saamri/Samri proved to be a popular monster, as **PURANA MANDIR** was a huge box office blockbuster for the Ramsays. The film should have been the Indian answer to Freddy Krueger, Michael Myers, or Jason Voorhees. But this the loose follow-up was way off the mark, and, no matter how cool the monster was, or how effective the stereoscopic effects were, something just didn't click and the ball was dropped…with a resounding *THUD*.

Instead of a direct sequel, where the creature of Saamri somehow manages to survive being skewered with a holy *trishula*, in **3D SAAMRI** we instead have an otherwise unrelated creature—whose name "just happens" to be Saamri—going on a killing spree. As the film opens, we are introduced to a man by the name of Dharmesh Saxena (Anirudh Agarwal, made-up to appear ancient in a bushy white wig), an old and powerful practitioner of white magic. He is a good man who worships the fierce black goddess Mata Devi Kaali, and, through his devotion and the use of benevolent magic, he helps needy folks in his small, close-knit community. His nickname "just happens" to be Saamri, and he later turns into a monster; but that's about the sole tenuous connection with **PURANA MANDIR**. Hence, a missed opportunity, to say the least!

However, on with the tale of Old Man Saamri… Dharmesh Saxena is a rich old fart, but is in ill health, and he suffers a devastating heart attack after conducting a particularly intense and strenuous magic ritual during which he expels a stubborn demon from a young woman. Dharmesh realizes the end is nigh, and he calls for his lawyer to draw up his will, planning on leaving his entire estate to a niece, Anju Trivedi (actress Aarti Gupta, who had costarred in **PURANA MANDIR**), who barely knows him. However, a group of conniving relatives and their assorted crooked close friends decide to beat the old man to death and dump his body in the local river, then they invite Anju to stay at her recently late uncle's mansion. Once there they will also gang up and kill her too, so that the vast fortune will go to Dharmesh's duplicitous cousin, "The Professor". Of course, they didn't count on the fact that Dharmesh was a much-loved figure in the community, or that his faithful servant Bhisham (the late actor Jack Guad, who usually plays the villain), also a practitioner in magic, would dig up his master's body and reanimate it. Bhisham, who witnessed the brutal murder of his beloved master, delivers the body to the old man's underground grotto, which is hidden in a secret chamber beneath his mansion. There Bhisham lays the rotting corpse out before a statue of Kaali and proceeds to slit the throat of a sacrificial black goat adorned with flowers, whereupon Bhisham collects the animal's blood in a chalice. He then pours this thick ichor onto the mouth of the deceased Dharmesh as he lies lifeless upon the altar. While chants of "*Saamri! Saamri! Saamri!*" are heard on the film's soundtrack (which, by the way, is one of the Ramsays' better ones), the body

---

2 The Hindi word *Saamri* / सामरी has puzzled me for a while now. As far as I can tell, it can be used as either a regular noun or a proper noun. From the usages I have seen, it translates as "magician", "wizard", "immortal", or variations thereof…sort of. But I have yet to find a properly verified translation. As a name, Saamri has shown up in past Indian fantasy films. The earliest reference I could locate was a character in the 1955 fantasy adventure film **ABE-HAYAT** (D: Ramanlal Desai). In this Ali-Babaesque adventure, Saamri is a magic-welding villain; although nowhere near as evil as the monster from **PURANA MANDIR** is.

HERE'S SKULL IN YER EYE! Saamri wields a stereoscopic staff to exorcise a young woman —and poke the audience in the eye!

of the old man shudders then rises up to exact some much-needed and well-deserved vengeance on those who had wronged him in life, and now, after his death, must forfeit their own lives in recompense.

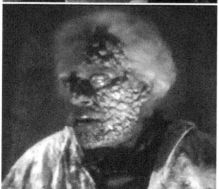

Anirudh Agarwal as the good magician, Dharmesh (**top**), who becomes the murderous vengeful monster, Saamri (**above**)

thereafter Dharmesh is thus reborn—dead/alive!—as the deliverer of supernatural retribution down on the wrongdoers' heads, and his monstrous, pustulent-mugged alter-ego Saamri then spends the remaining 90 minutes of the film lumbering around his former palatial abode, knocking-off those murderously obnoxious relatives of his and their cohorts. The plus-side of having an undead wizard as avenger (this part I thought was grand!) is that, besides crushing the heads of his victims, Saamri is also able to utilize magic. For instance, he magically spirits a woman out of a well down which she was hiding so he can throttle her. Elsewhere, the monster also levitates a car and spins it in the air (which is reminiscent of a scene from the 1978 Ramsay film **DARWAZA**). When the last villain is slain, the monster returns to the grotto and there, at the feet of Kaali's statue, Saamri deactivates himself/itself in a very nice and tidy fashion. His body is once again buried...possibly to be called on again to right further wrongs in future?

Sadly, that didn't happen. So what was the reason for this non-action on the part of the filmmakers? Did **3D SAAMRI** fail to scare up any real profits at the box office? This was a golden opportunity for the Ramsays to seriously develop their own name-brand monster; their very own Freddy, Jason, or Michael, so to speak. But that idea was buried along with the film's Saamri character, which was too bad as it was a truly original *Indian* monster, unlike those in the **DRACULA** (a.k.a. **HORROR OF DRACULA**, 1958, UK) / **BANDH DARWAZA**[3] (1990) and the **A NIGHTMARE ON ELM STREET** (1988, USA) rip-off **MAHAKAAL** (1993) wannabes.

---

3 Granted the link between the Ramsay film and the Hammer **DRACULA** is somewhat tenuous, it is much more apparent in **MAHAKAAL**.

In **3D SAAMRI**, co-directors Tulsi and Shyam don't waste any opportunity to show off their use of the stereoscopic process. From the rather impressive opening credits to the various instances of knives, needles, flaming torches, flying furniture and so forth coming at the camera, the film looked like it would have been pretty fun had I been fortunate enough to get to watch it in its original theatrical format. As usual, much like it does for most of his brothers' other films, Gangu Ramsay's cinematography really shines, his lively usage of blues and reds imbuing **3D SAAMRI** with a magically phantasmagoric atmosphere. His color palette works well within the meager budget and for the location shots, especially when coupled with the practical effects by Baldev and Krishan Malik. The Maliks had a hand in creating imaginative effects for all sorts of Bollywood productions, from simple dissolves, double exposures and animated work in other Ramsay films, to slightly more complicated—and rarely done—traveling matte work (as seen in Babubhai Mistri's 1990 fantasy hit **HAATIM TAI**). Here they maintained an even quality of optical work which mainly involved the stereoscopics.

Actor Anirudh Agarwal's first casting in a Ramsay film was on the aforementioned **PURANA MANDIR** (1984, D: Tulsi & Shyam Ramsay), wherein he played Saamri, a sinister cabalistic—and cannibalistic—practitioner of the dark arts. His 6' 7" frame came in handy when a menacing figure was required to provide chills and thrills. With his thick features and deep, booming voice, he was a shoo-in for such parts, although his acting skills were less than impressive (but then he wasn't hired for his Shakespearean training!). **PURANA MANDIR** proved to be such a financial success for the Ramsays that Agarwal was brought back as Dharmesh a.k.a. Saamri. It's a surprise that his vampire character from their **BANDH DARWAZA** (1990 [see *M!* #3, p.49]) wasn't also called by that name to cash-in on both **PURANA MANDIR** and **3D SAAMRI** (instead, he was known as Nevla). In fact, the name "Saamri" stuck with the actor, and followed him through a few of his other roles. He appeared as other Saamris in an episode of the Ramsay TV show *The Zee Horror Show* in 1996, as well as in the ghostly horror film **MALLIKA** (2010, D: Wilson Louis).

Agarwal has been typecast ever since; an actor who could have been used better by other directors, but never was. Most of his genre film work relied on his shambling around the set in full-on monster makeup, or stomping folks playing a thug, as seen in the AMeetabh Bachchan crime drama **AAJ KA ARJUN** (1990, D: K.C. Bokadia). He portrayed an evil *tantrik* in the 1990 *Nagin*/cobra woman film **TUM MERE HO** (D: Tahir Hussain [see *Weng's Chop* #3, p.84]), and he did a fine job

with the script that was handed to him. Agarwal managed to turn a few heads with his fleeting role as Babu Gujjar in the controversial action film **BANDIT QUEEN** (1994, D: Shekhar Kapur), and he also popped up in cameos as a *tantrik* in Dinesh K. Thakkar's horror comedy **DULHAN BANI DAYAAN** (1999), and as a brutish Naga tribesman named "Junglee" in **JOURNEY BOMBAY TO GOA: LAUGHTER UNLIMITED** (2007,

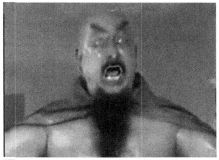

Years after the Ramsay flicks **PURANA MANDIR** (1984) and 3D **SAAMRI** (1985), the name of Saamri (or Samri, depending on how you transliterate it) must've still resonated in the minds of Bollywood audiences, as it seems to pop up frequently in other horror films. **Top:** A shot of the evil green-skinned *djinn* that was featured in *The Zee Horror Show* episode entitled "Saamri". **Above:** A "Grade C" horror film made in 2000 by Kanti Shah rival K.I. Sheikh; which has nothing whatsoever to do with the original Ramsay production, although it is fairly entertaining nonetheless

from the aforementioned **MAHAKAAL** (see *M!* #2, p.37). At least **3D SAAMRI** shares some of the cool alienness which makes Kiran Ramsay's **SHAITANI ILAAKA** (1990 [see *M!* #8, p.5]) such a delight to behold, though. Had more of an emphasis been placed on Saamri's ritualistic re-animation and the manner in which the monster stalked its victims, then I would have been one very happy camper indeed. But...*next!*

AAKHRI CHEEKH
(a.k.a. **THE FINAL SCREAM**)
India, 1991. D: Kiran Ramsay

AAKHRI CHEEKH (*"Scream of Death"*) was a Ramsay monster film cut from a slightly cheaper piece of cloth than their usual productions were. Maybe in '90 the family blew their whole annual budget on **BANDH DARWAZA** (see *M!* #3, p.49), or it could simply be that Kiran's **SHAITANI ILAAKA** (see *M!* #8, p.5) that same year didn't turn a profit, like his brothers Shyam's and Tulsi's films usually did. I'm not sure of the reason, but **AAKHRI CHEEKH** definitely does have the look and feel of a quickie toss-off to it. That said, this is yet another fine example of zilch-budget filmmaking, which I have a weakness/fondness for.

D: Raj Pendurkar; a remake of the 1972 film of the same name which was "loosely based on" [i.e., ripped-off from] Stanley Kramer's zany cult comedy "scavenger hunt" classic **IT'S A MAD, MAD, MAD, MAD WORLD** [1963, USA]). Agarwal's most widely-seen screen appearance in the West was his small role in Stephen Sommers' 1994 adaptation of Rudyard Kipling's **THE JUNGLE BOOK** (for which Agarwal was again seen as a hulking villain, this time around named "Tabaqui"). He has since retired from films.

The less said about a few of the other actors, the better! The comedian Jagdeep's absurd character Changez "*Star Trek*" Khan, the family cook who serves up coffee with a dog bone stirring stick, seriously undermines the shivers and shakes that Saamri the monster generates. I watched slack-jawed when Jagdeep stepped out with some funky zombies in full Michael Jackson "Thriller" attire (red jacket, "afro", and—*gulp*—blackface!) for a shitty fantasy dance number by Bappi Lahiri, complete with horrible "special" makeup effects that could easily be bested by most preteens on Halloween night. Only Jack Guad as Bhisham seems to really stand out among all the surrounding nonsense in this film.

As a whole I can say that I enjoyed **3D SAAMRI** for what it was: a mindless monster mash which should have had more onscreen appearances of the titular walking dead avenger. I'm a sucker for black magic, zombies, and alternate approaches to non-Western horror. Give me a *tantrik* magician raising corpses or calling for a demon any day over the ridiculous Freddy Krueger-like Shakaal

Kiran doesn't waste any time getting into the horror of the plot, as we are witness to a scene of black magic right within the first five minutes. As the credits roll, a hulking figure in rags is seen skulking through a Christian graveyard. This misshapen "person" stops in front of a gravesite, where a body is wrapped in a burial cloth. Lightning flashes, and we see that the figure is—*a monster!* Said thing—with deep-set eyes, a deformed, bulging forehead with a vacant "third eye" aperture, and large canine fangs—unwraps the body of a young woman from the cloth, slits her throat, then drains her blood from a neck wound into a chalice. The monster, named Nagi (Surendra Pal), who is a practitioner of the dark arts, raises the cup and pours the contents over his head. In typical Ramsay fashion, titillation and terror is intertwined, and, at the same moment that the corpse mutilation is occurring, a young woman elsewhere is shown taking a shower and readying herself for her lover...who happens to be Nagi! He arrives, and, in the midst of their love play, attacks her. She defensively grabs a gun from her nightstand and shoots him, but he transforms into the demonic creature he had been previously and strangles her. The monster then proceeds to drag her body down the stairs and outside the bungalow.

AAKHRI CHEEKH then introduces its four main characters—Rahul (Vijayendra Ghatge),

Jeet (Javed Khan), Samuel (Deepak Parashar) and Anand (Anil Dhawan)—who are best friends. They are a happy bunch and party together along with their and their significant others (wives, girlfriends, sisters—it's hard to tell sometimes in an Indian film without subtitles). We are also made aware—not that we didn't know already—that Nagi the evil black magician loves to woo young women, only to then transform into the aforementioned demonic monster in order to kill them during his ungodly rituals. However, he makes the mistake of attacking Jennifer David (Poonam Das Gupta), the sister of one of the men. Nagi chases her through a forest then a graveyard, and eventually into the arms of her protective brothers. After a violent struggle, the monster (now in human form) is subdued, arrested, and locked up for the murders of numerous women. However, after killing a guard and lifting his keys, the devilish, never-surrender Nagi escapes from his cell and makes his way back to the house to finish what he started. Apparently, Jennifer is worth him going out of his way to kill, but eventually he is shot and recaptured. Due to the extent of his crimes, Nagi is tried and sent to the (really rinky-dink!) electric chair.

Strapped into said execution device, Nagi threatens to return from Hell and kill 'em all! The switch is flipped and the punitive electrocution is carried out. As the deadly high-voltage surges through the vile warlock's body, he once again begins to change into the monster with disfigured facial features, fangs and all. No one seems to notice this rather startling development, however, as if they were more than half expecting the demon to erupt from within the man's body upon his execution. Of course, at this point anything that might have charitably been considered original was tossed out the window, and they simply lifted elements from Wes Craven's tongue-in-cheek horror film **SHOCKER** (1989, USA) to spice-up their own. To some degree, this "post-execution monster runs amok" plot had already popped up in the Lon Chaney, Jr./Jack Pollexfen horror film **INDESTRUCTIBLE MAN** (1956, USA), which itself was a partial variation of Chaney, Jr.'s and George Waggner's **MAN MADE MONSTER** (a.k.a. **THE ELECTRIC MAN**, 1941, USA). Granted, in that '56 low-budgeter Chaney's return from beyond the grave was accomplished using "science" and technology rather than via magical means, but the end-result was still *supernatural*, nonetheless, as he was playing a literal dead man walking, if a lot less mucked-up than the blistered, unnaturally sustained Nagi here.

Despite being physically deceased, the evil spirit of **AAKHRI CHEEKH**'s warlock lives on, whereafter he begins his retributory killing spree by hijacking a jeep, and nails a police guard to a wall as he is preparing a cross to mark the killer's grave. After the sharp-eyed local doctor notices something *odd* in an X-ray, it becomes abundantly clear that the killer isn't about to stay dead and buried. In fact, Nagi returns to take possession of the busty, lusty Meeta (played by the actress known as simply Sripradha), who proceeds to off said doctor before he can reveal that the killer just might—*gee, d'ya think?!*—still be very much "alive" (well, *kinda*). Meeta can also transform into the demon, and does so, attacking and killing Jeet's mother. Then she tops all that off by going on to murder her husband John, as well.

Sadly, at this point in the film, comedy—whether we want it or not—*has* to be introduced, and thereafter everything begins its slow but inexorable slide down into all-out crappiness. A goofy private investigator (Rajendra Nath, a well-known comedian) arrives on the scene accompanied by a sexy sidekick (Seema Vaz). Every time he appears on the screen, a swingin' Bollywood rip-off of Henry Mancini's *Pink Panther* theme is played. This horribly annoying—and then some—character is tossed into the plot at absurdly inopportune moments without really adding anything to the story. By now I suppose I should be used to these irritating "comic" interruptions to Indian films' plots…but I will *always* hate them!

The killings continue as the monster stalks Father Robert (Sujit Kumar), the local Catholic priest who was witness to the execution, and murders him in the cemetery by shoving a cross-shaped grave marker through is body. Subsequently, Jeet approaches a local Hindu priest (Kamal Kapoor) for help. Meanwhile, the demon assumes Jeet's physical form and attacks Jenny while she is bathing at the beach, biting her on the neck. She faints, and the monster vanishes. Jeet and the *baba* investigate the graveyard, where they discover the

The grisly visage of the monstrous wizard Rajesh from **AAKHRI CHEEKH**. Say what you must against the "cheapness" of a Ramsay horror film, but they had the best monsters in all of Bollywood

monster's black magic lair. The holy man explains that Jeet must locate the mark of evil on Jenny and Priya. This, of course, means that Jeet—and we, too—are given ample opportunities for peeping at the women while they bathe, and sneaking into their bedrooms to undress them physically while they sleep. Of course, this doesn't go over well with the rest of the gang, and Jeet gets smacked around some. However, it's only when the demon possesses another in the group and he attacks Priya that everyone comes onboard with Jeet. They all race to the graveyard, where the murderer is buried, and the holy man explains again that Nagi the *shaitan* can only be destroyed if they dig up the warlock's body and cremate it. They then begin to demolish Nagi's diabolic shrine with a magical battle-axe, but his acting earthly vessel Meeta attacks, having been drawn to the graveyard by the warlock's malevolent influence. Each blow of the axe against the unholy idol causes Meeta to writhe in pain, and, in a fairly grisly scene for a Ramsay film, the coalesced lump of palpable evil possessing her pops out from her belly. At the same time, the corpse springs to life and kills the holy man. Luckily, Rahul has brought along a handy flamethrower, and, *à la* the brain-slurping fiend in Chano Urueta's Mexploitation mega-classic **THE BRAINIAC** (*El barón del terror*, 1961), the evil entity is thus reduced to smoldering ashes.

AAKHRI CHEEKH plays like a veritable who's who of Bollywood fright flicks. In fact, many of the actors and actresses who appeared in this film made their living starring in many cheap horror, thriller and action films, and they have typically worked together on dozens of productions. Anil Dhawan and Javed Khan are two very familiar faces to those of us who have sat through numerous low-budget Bollywood genre movies, as I have. Anil Dhawan starred in the Ramsays' **PURANI HAVELI** (1989), **TERI TALASH MEIN** (1990, D: Vinod Talwar), him known only as Baby's—pronounced Babby—classic **PATHIMOONAM NUMBER VEEDU** (a.k.a. **HOUSE NO. 13**, 1991 [see *Weng's Chop* #4.5, p.117]), **AJOOBA KUDRAT KAA** (1991 [see *M!* #3, p.51]), P. Chandrakumar's excellent witch shocker **CHUDAIL** (1997 [see *WC* #0, p.48]), and even in the ultra-cheap R. Mittal horror flick **DAAK BANGLA** ([2000] a film that has nothing whatsoever to do with the classic 1987 Keshu Ramsay mad mummy film of the same name [see *M!* #2, p.39]). Javed Khan began his horror film affiliation in a string of Mohan Bhakri films, including **CHEEKH** (1985), **KHOONI MAHAL** (1987), **KABRASTAN** (1988), and **KHOONI MURDAA** (a.k.a. **DEADLY CORPSE**, 1989), also costarring Sripradha, before landing his co-lead role in **AAKHRI CHEEKH**. Khan would later find fame as a popular television actor, appearing in episodes of *The Zee Horror Show, Nagin* (an-

other Ramsay TV horror series), *The Ramayana* (a mythological series), and he's still working today (although his IMDb filmo stops dead at 2009). Sripradha, who plays Meeta, starred with Javed Khan in Vinod Talwar's totally awesome witch film **HATYARIN** (1991 [see *M!* #1, p.3]); they also appeared in the episode "Raat" from *The Zee Horror Show*, as well as being paired together in the horror films **KHOONI MURDAA** (1989) and **ROOHANI TAAQAT** (1991), both of which were directed by Mohan Bhakri; as well as in **MAJBOOR LADKI** (1991, D: Ram Pahwa) and **DAAYEN** (1997, D: Jagdish Gautam). Seema Vaz had a short career in Bollywood horror and action films which included roles in Kanti Shah's **GANGA JAMUNA KI LALKAAR** (1991 [see *WC* #5, p.183]), also appearing with Anil Dhawan in Vinod Talwar's **KHOONI PANJA** (1991 [see *M!* #10, p.5]), and again with Dhawan in **ANDHERA** (1994, D: Ajit Asthana), as well as appearing in **AADHI RAAT** (1999, D: Hriday Shankar). Surendra Pal played a *tantrik* in Kiran Ramsay's **SHAITANI ILAAKA** (1990 [see *M!* #8, p.5], which also starred Sripradha), tangled with a female ghost in **CHUDAIL KI RAAT** (2000, D: Dinesh Thakkar), and was in a few episodes of *The Zee Horror Show* as well, but seemed to have escaped being too tightly pigeonholed, although he did appear in two later Ramsay duds, **DHUNH: THE FOG** (2003) and **BACHAO – INSIDE BHOOT HAI...** (2010). He has since landed some choice parts in popular Indian TV shows. I could go on from there, but it would get even more complicated, to a point where you can almost play a game of "Six Degrees of **AAKHRI CHEEKH**"; so I'd better stop right now.

On a rather minor but interesting point, supporting actress Shehnaz Khan had a short-lived career as a "bombshell" and starred in bizarre Pakistani films like **HASEENA ATOM BOMB** (1990, D: Saeed Ali Khan) and the killer kitty critter flick **DA KHWAR LASME SPOGMAY** ("*The Cat-Beast*", 1997, D: Shehnaz Begum) before fading away into obscurity.

To wrap up, believe it or not, it looks like *Monster!* may be reaching the final films in the Ramsays' monstrous canon. In issue #15 (or maybe 16), look for reviews of their classic horror films **DARWAZA** (a.k.a. **THE DOOR**, 1978) and **VEERANA** (a.k.a. **VENGEANCE OF THE VAMPIRE** or **THE WILDERNESS**, 1989). Until then, feel free to expand your knowledge of internationally-made monster movies by going to YouTube and typing in "Bollywood Horror Films", just to see what you come up with. *Enjoy!*

BUYING IN BULK
Adding the Unusual and Obscure to your video library

As crummy as most of these films are with their lame monsters, I have come to appreciate them for what they are: examples of almost pure Cinema. There is a popular catch-all term that is bandied about by critics: "Outsider" cinema. This oft-coined term comes from the equally popular Outsider art scene involving artists who create without any formal training whatsoever. Similar to the *Art Brut* and naïve "folk" scene that triggered excitement in the art world during the early 1960s and '70s (an art movement whose lineage can be traced back to the insane asylum inmate art which began to be collected back in the 1920s and '30s). For all intents and purposes, these films could very well fit right into that movement.

Then you could also approach them on a totally different level; that of an alternate reality. In this realm of existence, the world is populated by scandalously clad young women who are being stalked by lecherous, sex-crazed men as well as by supernatural creatures. These entities might enter our reality by forming themselves into what could be commonly called cheap rubber Halloween costumes. It is the closest that we can get to understanding the nature of their being.

Okay, that's a little far-fetched, but considering that no one has ever seen a demon or alien or such a monster, then, for all we know, some *thing* could very well look like a crappy trick-or-treater. Or maybe even Hello Kitty.

Earlier films, like the werewolf movie **JANNI DUSHMAN** (1979), and **MANGALSUTRA** (1981), with its spiritual possession theme, were essentially made for wider audience appeal, although their distribution was severely hampered by censorship and outright bans. Other horror films were part of this movement in the late '70s and early '80s, echoing the nontraditional, influential Western terrors, albeit spiced with Indian flavor. These were expensive endeavors that took too long to make and didn't play well in some of the seedier theaters. The exploitation of the sleaze-hungry lower-class was just around the corner, and the popular horror/sex mash-up of the '90s was brewing, ready to be served…

At this point in the New Millennium, "6-in-2-Super DVD" packs are fairly commonplace, and can be a good method for collecting a vast catalog of films without exerting too much energy. For the most part, companies tend to have genre-based anthologies covering such genres as horror, sexy, action, mythological, drama, historical, comedy and so on.

Buying one or more of these collections may be ideal for those of you who don't like VCDs (which are notoriously buggy). Companies, like Moser Baer Entertainment (one of India's largest producers of home video), do offer DVD collections of the more obscure titles. As popular as this format is, the visual quality suffers immensely. Imagine cramming three 120- to 160-minute movies onto one single-layer disc. That's a *lot* of compression, and digital artifacts do pop up frequently. But six films for $2.50 is still a bargain, even if their transfers don't merit that "Super DVD" hype promised by the sleeve art. Their source material is pretty much the same as the VCDs; some even are widescreen, if that matters. For those of you who might be wondering, these are threadbare DVDs, with no bonus material whatsoever—no trailers, no subtitles, no documentaries or commentaries. Just the movies.

(This originally appeared in Weng's Chop #1, and has been edited and updated here.)

ATTACK!!!

Reviewed by Stephen R. Bissette

Monster Attack Team magazine #11 (2015) is just out, for just $11.00—bargain-priced, given its jam-packed 80+ pages of full-color interviews, articles, and retrospectives. Beneath a glorious "Save the Earth!" cover by outstanding cover artist Jolyon Yates (who has more than made his indelible mark on the current zine scene multiple times, and no doubt will continue to, including some memorable Weng's Chop *covers), editors Edward L. Holland and M.G. Keller have packaged a plethora of delights for* daikaijū-eiga *devotees, manga maniacs, and Japanese pop music listeners with long memories.*

Since Greg Shoemaker pioneered this vein of pop culture research with his then-innovative fanzine *Japanese Fantasy Film Journal*, there's been a healthy and almost ceaseless stream of English-language Japanese pop culture lovefests in print. While most of these have singular focal points—Godzilla and/or Toho monster movies, manga, anime, etc.—*Monster Attack Team* has managed over its lifespan to expand from its original *tokusatsu* monster-bashing interests to something richer and deeper. This Ka-Blam-printed issue furthers that evolution nicely, maintaining the warmth and enthusiasm of co-founders Holland and (the late) Joe Riley's original issues while stretching the scope and (now slick) look and feel of every issue. The intimacy is still visible, and Holland's personal touch is felt throughout. Holland himself most

respectfully interviews manga/anime master Leiji Matsumoto (of **SPACE BATTLESHIP YAMATO** [宇宙戦艦ヤマト / *Uchū Senkan Yamato* /, 1974], **SPACE PIRATE CAPTAIN HARLOCK** [宇宙海賊キャプテンハーロック / *Uchū Kaizoku Kyaputen Hārokku*] and **GALAXY EXPRESS 999** [銀河鉄道999 / スリーナイン / *Ginga Tetsudō Surī Nain*, both 1977], etc.) and *Kamen Rider Amazon* (仮面ライダーアマゾン / *Kamen Raidā Amazon*)'s star Toru Okazaki (the shortest and most violent of all the *Kamen Rider* shows [1974-75]). You can feel the love radiate from the pages!

#11 is a feast for open eyes and minds. There's a procession of heavily-illustrated articles herein spiced with a number of first-person insider surprises. Brad Warner's memories of working for Tsuburaya Productions (including a stretch during their lean years) lends considerable context and weight to Fabien Mauro's more traditionally-scribed look at Eiji Tsuburaya's special effects career, culminating in the launch and success of Tsuburaya Productions in the final decade of Eiji's life. Mauro folds into his essay some off-the-cuff proselytizing for the relatively unloved **GODZILLA RAIDS AGAIN** (ゴジラの逆襲 / *Gojira no Gyakushū*, a.k.a. **GIGANTIS THE FIRE MONSTER** [1955]), which nicely anticipates and sets the tone for the cover articles. The one-two punch into Hedorah himself/itself is the heart of this particular issue. The first "punch" is Christian Divine's retrospective look at Yoshimitsu Banno's **GODZILLA VS. HEDORAH** (ゴジラ対ヘドラ / *Gojira tai Hedora*, a.k.a. **GODZILLA VS. THE SMOG MONSTER** [1971]), springboarding from Divine's memories of first seeing the film into a thorough overview of its conception, production, and Toho's less-than-enthusiastic reaction to Banno's radical, inventive revamping of the franchise. By way of constructive criticism, however, I must note that Divine misses some of the more obvious ways that Hedorah has rippled through international pop culture: consider, for instance, world-renowned cartoonist Panter isn't exactly an obscure reference point, especially in Japan (after all, how many American cartoonists have a coffee shop in Nagoya named after them and using their artwork and designs?). Well, that's OK: nobody in comics fandom or academia seems to have picked up on Panter adopting Hedorah for his comics, either! Divine's loving essay is followed by editor Edward L. Holland's sober "Hedorah, Harbinger of Hedoro", tracing how Japan's previous, then-contemporary, and subsequent real-world pollution scares, atrocities, and case histories informed the creation and legacy of Hedorah, "the Smog Monster". Without derailing the pop vibe of *Monster Attack Team*'s imperative, Holland's comparatively introspective science-based coda to Divine's *Gojira tai Hedora* puts some meat on the zine's bones.

Then again, *fun* is the focus, what with Damon Foster's memories—and photos!—of his visit (with Ed Martinez) to the set of Toei's *tokusatsu* TV series *Special Megabeast Investigator Juspion* (巨獣特捜ジャスピオン / *Kyojū Tokusō Jasupion* [1985-86]) illuminating 4 pages after M.G. Keller's overview of the show itself, lending some welcome context for the uninitiated. Andy B. provides an overview of Super Festival 64 (the *tokusatsu* toy fair), Gentleman John Battles offers a compelling and lengthy article on the group Golden Cups from the 1960s+, and sage Toho expert Ed Godziszewski lends an ear to the legacy of the Toho monster sound effects and how they were created. All in all, this is another eye-popping, entertaining, and most informative treat for those of you who (like me) love this subject matter. Highest recommendation!

(To order, go to *http://www.indyplanet.com/front/product/114322/* or *http://www.monster-attackteam.com/magazine/* for print or online copies; see *http://www.facebook.com/MATfightmonsters* for more info).

Hooray For Hedorah! **Top:** Gary Panter's adoption of Hedorah for his cover art for the 1979 Frank Zappa album, *Sleep Dirt.* **Center:** And as "Smoggo", Jimbo's sidekick in *Raw* #6 (1983). **Bottom:** US pressbook advert for the oddest (in a good way) Godzilla film in the series' 50-year run, and the only 'Zilla film made by one-off director Yoshimitsu Banno (坂野義光). Pity he didn't make more of them!

OUT OF POLLUTION'S DEPTHS IT SLITHERS!
Breathing Poison... Leaving a wake of deadly slime...
Destroying all in its path!

GODZILLA VS. THE SMOG MONSTER

COLOR by MOVIELAB · IN COLORSCOPE
G-28
An American International Release

MONSTER! #14 MOVIE CHECKLIST

MONSTER! Public Service posting: Title availability of films reviewed or mentioned in this issue of MONSTER!
Information dug up and presented by Steve Fenton and Tim Paxton.

*The Fine Print: Unless otherwise noted, all Blu-rays and DVDs listed in this section are in the NTSC Region A/Region 1 format and widescreen, as well as coming complete with English dialogue (i.e., were either originally shot in that language, or else dubbed/subbed into it). If there are any deviations from the norm, such as full-frame format, discs from different regions or foreign-language dialogue (etc.), it shall be duly noted under the headings of the individual entries below.

One of a few "3in1 DVD" collections
featuring **3D SAAMRI**

3D SAAMRI (p.85) – A highly watchable upload of the film—complete with English subtitles, yet (*bonus!*)—can be found on YouTube at the link simply entitled "Saamri" (at *https://www.youtube. com/watch?v=X-P4-YZIuL8*), so be sure to have your *savefrom.net* downloader ready! According to the IMDb, the film's full-length running time is 102m, which is quite short for an Indian film. That said, the English-subbed rip at YT runs even shorter (just a few seconds over 94½ minutes). It was formerly evidently put out on VCD (and VHS tape?) by Raj Video, and also issued in the same disc format by both Kamal Video and on the Priya label. For the asking price of Rs.38 (that's in rupees), copies of that lattermost version are currently in stock at Induna (*www.induna.com*); you might also want to check on *bhavanidvd.com* too; we couldn't find a listing for it when we did a search there, however. For Rs.49, Induna also offers it in a 3-film, 1-disc DVD (also from Priya), triple-billed with a pair of other Hindi hor-

ror flicks: The Ramsays' **VEERANA** and Mohan Bhakri's **KABRASTAN** (both 1988). So far as we know, none of the aforementioned versions other than for that YT rip come with English subs. Although in its "flat" (i.e., 2D) version this film is commonly known simply as **SAAMRI** (as on all those disc editions we mentioned here), it should not be confused with another cheap Hindi horror of the same name from the year 2000, directed by K.I. Sheikh. Starring Jyoti Rana and Gajendra Chouhan, that film is available on Moser Baer/ Aduk Home Entertainment and Captain VCD.

13 EERIE (p.43) – Ad-line: *"We Prey For You"*. Available on domestic DVD from Entertainment One. It can also be rented/purchased as an Amazon Instant Video in either the HD or SD quality formats (for $2.99/$12.99 in the former and $1.99/$9.99 in the latter). It still regularly pops up as token Can-con padding on Canuck cable too. We're pretty sure it's streamable VOD all over the 'net, so those who want it know where to look for it.

AAKHRI CHEEKH (p.90) – Formerly available in Hindi (sans English) on VCD from Moser Baer; as of this writing, said disc was listed as being out of stock at Induna (*www.induna.com*). AC was also included in a "3in1" DVD (likewise from Moser Baer?), triple-billed with two other Hindi horror films: D. Mansukh Lal's **LAASH** (1998), starring Chandni Gupta and Kirti Rawal; and Hemant Kamal's **KAALA MANDIR** (2000), starring Neelam Sagar and Shakti Kapoor. Only a couple longish excerpts of the present title appear to be uploaded to YouTube, but they do include some key horror elements, so check 'em out (one's located at the link titled "Aakhri cheekh (adult) part-7 horror movie for18+ only"). It goes without saying that this 1991 film should not be confused with two other Hindi horrors: namely Mohan Bhakri's **CHEEKH** (a.k.a. **THE SCREAM**, 1985), nor Kanti Shah's **CHEEKH** (2004), a ghostly possession shocker starring super-stacked sex bomb Sapna (see *Weng's Chop #5*), its director's wife. Incidentally, full-length versions of both **CHEEKH**s are uploaded to YT. Neither of them come with English subs either.

ALIEN LOCKDOWN (p.54) – Ad-line: *"It's Time To Prey"*. Available on domestic DVD from Millennium, and also as an insta-vid on Amazon, albeit only in Standard Definition (SD) quality format ($2.99 to rent, $4.99 to buy).

AMERICAN WARSHIPS (p.55) – Put out on domestic Blu-ray and DVD in 2012 by The Asylum Home Entertainment. Let's just say that, judging by shots we've seen of the movie's exceedingly goofy/foolish-looking CG alien invaders (take a look on p.55, if you don't believe us!), it comes as no surprise to us at all that they don't reveal them in the trailer, which instead mostly concentrates on the heavy-hitting firepower of the title naval vessels.

ANDROID APOCALYPSE (p.58) – On Magnolia Home Entertainment DVD, who also released it in a "Widescreen Extended Version". The film is alternately available as an Amazon insta-vid in the SD-only format, either to rent (for $2.99) or buy ($9.99).

BLACULA & SCREAM BLACULA SCREAM (pp.34-41) – Issued as a Blu-ray double-bill by Shout! Factory as part of their Scream Factory horror-oriented off-shoot line. Back in 2009, both films were also released in conjunction by 20th Century Fox as a 2-disc DVD set in their "Soul Cinema" series (cover-blurb: *"That Brother's Bite Was Outta Sight!"*). Earlier (in 2004), Fox also issued the pair separately on DVD as part of the same series. The duo are currently available for rental or purchase as Amazon insta-vids (both SD-only for either $2.99 to rent or $9.99 to buy), so why not sink your teeth into 'em today?!

DEADLY EYES (p.56) – In 2014, this long-un-seen-and-unsung Canuxploitation mutant rodent movie was made available as a Blu-ray/DVD Combo Pack from Shout! Factory. Waaaaayyy back in 1983, it was put out on domestic pan-and-scan VHS/Beta pre-record tape by Warner Home Video (encased in a clamshell box, as per many Warner releases of the time), and was also made available in the UK from Guild Home Video in the same formats (albeit in PAL rather than NTSC, natch) during the same period. As of this writing, a copy of said Warner VHS was up for sale on Amazon for around $35. But—unless you happen to have money to burn—why buy a much fuzzier full-frame copy at that price when you can pick up the crystal-clear Blu + DVD for only $25 or so instead? Shot in Toronto, **DE** includes shots of TO's Old City Hall and that world-famous tourist trap/consumerist mecca (i.e., place to avoid like rat poison or, better yet, the bubonic plague), the Eaton Centre, plus other local landmarks well-known to Torontonians too (albeit no shots of the CN Tower, however; that would be too much of a dead give-

away that the flick wasn't shot in Anywhere City, U.S. of A, like they're trying to imply). *See!* Babies and old people get, um, chewed all to ratshit! That said, while I was watching the scene wherein poor little unattended tot Caroline gets dragged out of her highchair and devoured—albeit thankfully sight unseen, securely off-screen—by hungry super-rodents while having her din-dins, the chorus of that early '80s *Oi!*core song "City Baby Attacked By Rats" by Brit punkers GBH kept running through my head. In keeping with director Robert Clouse's chop socky genre rep, at a Bruce Lee Retrospective in **DE**, clips from Clouse's (and co-director Sammo Hung's) posthumous Lee patchwork cash-grab **GAME OF DEATH** (死亡游戏 / *Si wang you xi*,

未確認エイリアン─出現！

THE DEADLY SPAWN

EATING MACHINE
デッドリースポーン

Japanese **THE DEADLY SPAWN** VHS tape

1978, Hong Kong/USA) are seen unreeling on a repertory cinema screen; namely, some of Bruce's and the towering Kareem Abdul-Jabbar's epic *mano a mano* fists'n'feets brawl therein. Like the present title, **GOD** (an apt acronym, BTW) was likewise a Golden Harvest co-production, providing still another direct connection. The scene here wherein the ravenous 'roided-up rats swarm panicking moviegoers in the theater's aisles and foyer is one of the gory action highpoints of the movie, as is the climactic sequence down in the subway tunnel of the bogus "State Street Station" (shooting sites c/o the TTC [Toronto Transit Commission]).

THE DEADLY SPAWN (p.61) – Alternate ad-lines: *"They Came To Earth To Feed On Human Flesh!"* and *"A Meteor Crashed On Earth... No One Knew The Mystery Of The Mutant Spores Inside!"* Released on domestic Blu-ray/DVD in a deluxe "Millennium Edition" by Elite Entertainment in 2012 (*"Earth vs. The Ultimate Eating Machine"*). That same year, it was also released on PAL Region 2 DVD by the UK's Arrow Video. That edition came with a reversible sleeve which included the original poster art on one side and stunning all-new artwork by Rick Melton on the other. Amongst other special features, Arrow's disc includes a thick souvenir booklet all about **DS**, written by Calum Waddell and Tim **"2001 MANIACS"** Sullivan; plus still *more* goodies besides! As per the film's original theatrical specs, all disc/tape versions are presented at a 1.33:1 (fullscreen) aspect ratio. In the '80s, **DS** was variously put out on domestic VHS and Betamax cassette by Cinema Group Home Video, LA's budget outfit Continental Video, as well as by NYC's Planet Video, Inc. In Canada, it was released on videocassette by both Video One (in

1985) and VEC (box-blurb: *"Mankind vs. The Ultimate Eating Machine"*). Also in the '80s, VIPCo (Video Instant Picture Company) issued it on videotape in the UK. In the Netherlands, Video For Pleasure put it out on tape, with English dialogue and Dutch subs. Much later (in 2004), Synapse Films released a Special Edition domestic DVD whose numerous extras included an alternate opening sequence, plus an outtakes reel and videotaped cast auditions (some of these same extras were later included with Arrow's aforementioned DVD edition). A trailer for the film is included on Synapse's preview compilation, **42ND STREET FOREVER**; in fact, an illustration of one of the spawn appears right in the comp's colorful Bluray cover artwork, along with one of the tentacle critters from **THE GREEN SLIME** (see *Monster!* #12, p.75); interestingly enough, a **SLIME** poster appears on the boy hero's bedroom wall in **SPAWN**. Under the title **KOSMOKILLER – SIE FRESSEN ALLES**, it was issued on PAL Region 2 DVD in Germany by X-Rated Kultvideo in 2010 (in the '80s, Toppic Polyband had released it on VHS/Beta in the same country). Whichever version you happen to be watching, keep an eye out for the cameo by Denis Gifford's seminal '70s tome *The Pictorial History of Horror Movies* in the scene where kid hero Charles Hildebrandt is first seen, watching a scary movie on a portable TV in his room. Naturally enough, an ish of *FM* pops up too, and its name is even dropped in passing (as are **THE MOLE PEOPLE** and **IT! THE TERROR FROM BEYOND SPACE!** Plus there are oodles of vintage monster movie posters on display in the background to some scenes, too). Michael Perilstein's electronic **DS** score was initially released in the US in 1985 as a vinyl LP by Deadly Records (#DS6041). Perseverance Records subsequently rereleased the soundtrack on CD/vinyl LP in 2004. Priced accordingly, it can currently be purchased in either of those formats or as MP3 files from Amazon (MP3: $8.99, CD: $18.17, LP: $29.98 [prices may vary depending on which link or site you source]). Punny track titles include: "All That Slithers Is Not Good", "Spawn With the Wind", "Let's Spawn", "Here Today, Spawn Tomorrow", "Spawn Lake" and "Spawn Who Came In from the Cold" (etc). In 2013, Mondo Records of Austin, TX. also issued a special remastered Limited Edition "pink" vinyl pressing of the soundtrack as a long-play (LP) record album enclosed in a spectacular, predominantly red gatefold sleeve swarming with gaping-jawed, titanic-toothed spawn (snazzy artwork c/o Phantom City Creative). Hell, Mondo rex representative Justin Ishmael is such a dedicated fan, he even has a **DS** tat! To order said disc, visit Discogs.com (*http://www.discogs.com/Michael-Perilstein-The-Deadly-Spawn-Original-Motion-Picture-Soundtrack/release/4198833*). Also, watch out for SPFX Comics Group's 2011 sequential art spinoff/tribute, *The Deadly Spawn*. In summation, it's easy to see why this lovely li'l ultra-low-budget "mom'n'pop" monster movie has gone on to have such a loyal cult following as it does. In this the age of largely synthetic and soulless computer-made critters, the all-natcheral, 100% bona fide practical FX seen herein really do have a lot of heart. Those wriggling polymorphous pollywogs ("nasty tadpoles") of varying sizes are especially effective, and in some shots appear truly alive, that's how organically fluid their movements are. Get **SPAWN**ed, or be scorned!

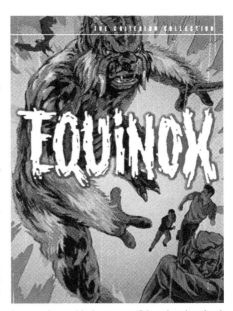

EQUINOX (pp.8-33) – Issued on DVD as part of the Criterion Collection in 2006. Their edition included both the quite drastically different original '67 cut of the film (entitled **THE EQUINOX...A JOURNEY INTO THE SUPERNATURAL**), as well as Jack H. Harris' and Jack Woods' considerably rearranged 1970 revision/reedit, which was released theatrically under the far-less-ungainly title of simply **EQUINOX**. The Criterion disc release's wealth of extras includes: a special video intro by *Famous Monsters* honcho Forrest J. Ackerman; two separate audio commentary tracks, one on **E** '70 by writer-director Woods and producer Harris and another on **E** '67 by co-creators Dennis Muren, Mark McGee and Jim Danforth; interviews with Muren and cast members Frank Bonner ("Jim"), Barbara Hewitt ("Susan") and James Duron (who played a looney-bin orderly in the film); deleted scenes and outtakes from the '67 version; archival stop-motion test footage; David Allen's famed sto-mo "Kong" TV commercial for Volkswagen's 411 model four-door sedan (narration: "So now there's a Volkswagen big enough for just about *everyone!*"), a spot originally produced for Cascade Pictures in 1972. In addition, the package includes Kevin Fernan's amateur (16mm?) silent short film, *Zorgon: The H-Bomb Beast from Hell* (1972, USA), which utilized **EQUINOX** personnel both behind and in front of the camera. No less than David Allen played its title "monster" (note quotes), whose costume utilized bits and pieces of Rick Baker's critter suits from Harry Essex's **OCTAMAN** (1971, USA [see *Monster!* #5, p.29]) and John Landis' **SCHLOCK** (a.k.a. **THE BANANA MONSTER**, 1972, USA). Minus the ape-head (which is here replaced by a goofy rubber mask, complete with ungainly "cheek-horns", white hair/beard and lopsided plastic vampire fangs), the upper body from the latter title creature was reused, as were the lower limbs (i.e., "leg tentacles") of the former. Hence, Zorgon is a real mishmash/chimera, for sure! **EQUINOX** FX man Danforth played one of the "posse" members in the short (basically, a bunch of "kids" go off hunting for the thing out in the wilderness). Much of the action was lensed in Bronson Canyon, where parts of **OCTAMAN** and many other even older monster movies were shot. Surprising-

ly enough considering some of the talent involved, the short is exceedingly statically paced and for the most part very ineptly put together (sorry, but it had to be said). Worst of all, it comes with a groaner "*Scooby-Doo*" ending of the lamest order, for shame! For some reason, McGee, Baker, Fernan, Allen and other participants all pose smiling proudly at the end, as if at a job well-done. Guess you had to be there. As for **EQUINOX**, in 2012, Umbrella Entertainment released the film on DVD in Australia. It was formerly available domestically in two different VHS/Betamax videocassette versions from Wizard Video, who originally put it out in those formats in 1981 under the present title in a standard "slipcase"-style box (#27 was printed on the spine), then subsequently (1985) reissued it in the same formats in a "big-box" edition (spine #63) under the title **THE BEAST**. Complete with a sealed-behind-clear-plastic wraparound insert of

Zorgon: The H-Bomb Beast from Hell

original promo art and encased in a sturdy plastic clamshell box, Vogue Video issued it on VHS/Beta in Canada *circa* the early '80s, but copies became pretty hard to come by (i.e., real rare). In the UK it was released on tape (in 1980) by Mountain Video, complete with crudely rendered wannabe Frank Frazetta/Val Mayerik-style cover art.

FLIGHT TO HELL (p.64) – Random dialogue exclamation: *"Holy shit!"* Holy shit indeed. FTH was issued on PAL Region 2 DVD in the UK by Prism Leisure Corporation in 2002. There are a few brief clips of this loony-toonz film uploaded to YouTube, for those who might want a bit of a taster before splurging on a copy of the disc (assuming you can find one, as it's presumably long out-of-print by now).

THE LAST FRANKENSTEIN (p.59) – As of this writing, the grey-to-black market site Japandown was offering an English-soft-subbed download of this film for sale (@ the page *http://www.japandownload.com/2014/11/the-last-frankenstein-1991-rasuto.html#.VN0oH_nF98F*). Sources for copies of this long-OOP title seem be few and far between (we couldn't even find it at Far East Flix), but there is an original Japanese video preview trailer viewable on YouTube at the link entitled "The Last Frankenstein Trailer (1991)" (*https://www.youtube.com/watch?v=BbP2j6fTEX0*) for those who want a teaser to decide whether it's worth tracking down and springing for a copy of the full movie or not. Surprisingly enough considering its cult following, the film hasn't even received any legit Japanese disc release yet, but presumably fan-subbed copies are floating around on DVD-R

somewhere out there. (Or maybe on Cinemageddon? Wouldn't know, ain't a member, don't wanna be.)

THE MONOLITH MONSTERS (p.68) – Included as one of the 10 titles in Universal Studios Home Entertainment's essential "The Classic Sci-Fi Ultimate Collection" Region 1 DVD box set, released in 2008 (both Volumes 1 & 2—six discs in total—came packaged together as a single unit in two separate clamshell boxes (with 3 discs apiece), all contained in a clear, snug-fitting plastic slipcase. Bold, colorful graphics make the package that much nicer!). The other 9 Universal-International science fiction/monster flicks comped with the present title are Jack Arnold's **THE INCREDIBLE SHRINKING MAN** (1957) and Edward Dein's non-SF'er **THE LEECH WOMAN** ([1960] both also starring Grant Williams [see *Weng's Chop* #6.5 for a review of that lattermost title]); along with Arnold's **TARANTULA** (1955) and **MONSTER ON THE CAMPUS** (1958), Nathan Hertz Juran's **THE DEADLY MANTIS** (1957), Virgil W. Vogel's **THE MOLE PEOPLE** (1956) and **THE LAND UNKNOWN** (1957), plus Francis D. Lyon's utterly non-science fictional, would-be Lewtonesque "horror" film **CULT OF THE COBRA** (1955); and, last but definitely not least, Ernest B. Schoedsack's prototypical "shrunken humans" thriller **DR. CYCLOPS** (1940), a film which was originally produced for Paramount Pictures, but (as with Erle C. Kenton's utterly fabulous **ISLAND OF LOST SOULS** [1932]) its rights subsequently became the property of Universal, hence that former title's inclusion with all these other U-I properties listed here. Although some of the films compiled in said set are lesser than others, it nonetheless amounts to a true must-have collection indeed for fans of '50s fantasy cinema in general and of the Universal universe in particular. Uni have also issued their "The Classic Sci-Fi Ultimate Collection" broken up into two separate 3-disc volumes, splitting the above-listed 10 titles into 5 per each set. All films are individually presented at whatever their original theatrical aspect ratio was (ranging from plain ol' fullscreen to various degrees of widescreen [i.e., 1.33:1, 1.78:1, 1.85:1 and 2.35:1]). As of this writing, copies of both those sets and the above-cited 10-film deluxe version were up for sale on Amazon and eBay. Prices vary sharply, so shop wisely. Better to get the entire 10-pack for cheaper than buying both 5-packs separately and paying more! (Well, *duuuhhhh!* ☺) As with all those other titles cited in this entry, **MM** was formerly (*circa* the early/mid-'90s) put out on VHS/Beta tape by MCA/Universal Home Video, although those releases—which were state-of-the-art at the time, with pristine transfer prints and pretty sharp picture quality—unfortunately presented everything in the full-frame format.

MONSTER IN THE CLOSET (p.52) – Issued onto DVD by Troma Entertainment back in 1998. It is currently up for rent (at $2.99) or purchase ($9.99) as an Amazon Instant Video, available in SD ("Standard Definition") quality mode only. A passable copy is viewable on YouTube (don't worry, Lloyd Kaufman won't mind: there's shitloads of officially free Troma shit plastered all over said site!).

PARASITE (p.72) – Laserdisc sleeve-blurbs: *"A ravenous terror from within... It slithers. It slides. It nibbles. It gnaws. It burrows through skin to set mind and body on fire. It's a PARA-SITE, and it's coming to get you"*. Released on domestic DVD by Anchor Bay Entertainment in 2002, it was previously put out on (full-screen?) DVD by Cult Video in '99. Prior to that (*circa* the early '90s), Shadow Entertainment released it on domestic laserdisc (catalogue #LV13001), albeit at an only 1.33:1 aspect ratio (unlike AB's aforementioned '02 DVD, which was widescreen [@ a full 2.35:1]). Consecutively and/or prior to said LD release, it was made available on N. American VHS/Beta cassette by both Embassy Home Entertainment and Paramount Home Video, as well as in the same oxide tape formats (possibly VHS only?) in the UK by the Entertainment In Video label. In roughly the same timeframe, it was apparently also put out on VideoDisc for the now-antiquated RCA SelectaVision system as a CED (Capacitance Electronic Disc). While I (i.e., SF) never saw this flick first-run (at least I *don't* think I did; me memory's vague) in its full three dimensions—it's been a "guilty pleasure" of mine for decades!—I do however recall seeing it a couple years after the fact at a pair of different Toronto grindhouses on the downtown Yonge Street drag; namely at the Coronet and the Rio, two sleazy skidrow shitholes that have long been out of business (if by no means good riddance to 'em!); for instance, somewhere around the mid/late-'80s, said Coronet became converted/homogenized into a secondhand jewelry exchange, of all things, albeit still retaining its original cinema handle (go figure). But back in their steadily waning "heydays", **PARASITE** seemed to be a staple title on these grindhouses' discount multi-bills, which, to the best of my recollection, typically offered three "beyond-first-run" movies at a mere $2.99 for the lot (prices tended to increase by increments from year to year to keep up with the rate of inflation). Other monster movies—often **ALIEN** rip-offs—I remember seeing at either/or of those aforementioned fleapits (or possibly at another TO grindhouse called The Biltmore, which was situated in much the same generally disreputable vicinity as the others) were Bill Malone's **SCARED TO DEATH** (1980 [to be reviewed by Eric Messina next ish!]) and **CREATURE** (a.k.a. **TITAN FIND**, 1985, both USA), such primo Rog Cor-

man/New World Pictures super-schlock as **HUMANOIDS FROM THE DEEP** (1980), **GALAXY OF TERROR** (1981) and **FORBIDDEN WORLD** (1982, all USA), Harry Bromley Davenport's offbeat E.T. invasioner **XTRO** (1982, UK), Jackie Kong's toxic waste mutant monster opus **THE BEING** (1983, USA), the Bands' own ghastly **GHOULIES** (1984, USA), plus many others whose titles I have long since forgotten, including numerous non-monster flicks too (e.g., drastically-censored, R-rated cutbacks of what were originally XXX American porn flicks were also frequent fodder on those establishments' marquees. For instance, I remember seeing a slashed-to-ribbons Ontario print of **DRACULA SUCKS** [see *Monster!* #6, p.66] there, and they didn't even leave in a single shot of John C. Holmes' main claim to fame!). However, I now return you to the present... A nifty trailer for the current title under discussion can be found at the YouTube link entitled "Parasite (1982) Trailer". The director's brother Richard Band's original score was put out on CD by the Intrada label as part of their Signature Editions series. Needless to say (but we will anyway), the present **PARASITE** should not be confused with Andrew Prendergast's 2004 British movie of the same name, about a monstrous marine creature preying on humans at a derelict North Sea oil rig.

THE PLAGUE OF THE ZOMBIES (p.77) – Made available in 2012 as a PAL Region B "Special Edition Double Play" Blu-ray/DVD combo from StudioCanal. It was formerly issued on domestic DVD by Anchor Bay Entertainment in 1999 (now OOP). Extras include: an episode of the *World of Hammer* doc series entitled "Mummies, Werewolves and the Living Dead", a trailer, and an insert card with a reproduction of the theatrical poster from when it was double-billed with **DRACULA – PRINCE OF DARKNESS** (see *Monster!* #13, p.27).

PARASITE laserdisc

THE REPTILE (p.79) – Made available in 2012 as a PAL Region B "Special Edition Double Play" Blu-ray/DVD combo from StudioCanal. According to Amazon, an NTSC Region A-format Blu edition was also released (in 2013). It was previously issued on domestic DVD by Anchor Bay Entertainment in 1999 (now OOP). Extras with that AB release include: An episode of *World of Hammer* entitled "Vamps", a trailer for a pair-up of the present title with **RASPUTIN – THE MAD MONK**, and a printed insert of the US theatrical poster for **REPTILE**'s double-bill

SPACE MILKSHAKE (p.46) – From what we can tell, it hasn't been released domestically in any digital disc format yet (?), but it is available

for rental or purchase as an Amazon insta-vid, in HD ($4.99/$12.99) or SD ($3.99/$9.99). The flick can also be purchased for $8 as a direct download at its official website (*www.spacemilkshake. com*). As director Armen Evrensel says in an open letter at that site, "*The movie is also about non-traditional relationships. Man/robot. Computer/robot. Woman/monster. Man/robot/duck. Duck/woman/duck/monster. Duck/duck/robot/ duck... The making of such a story could never happen by ordinary means. Major studios do not tell these stories. They don't know how to tell the story of the little guy, even if they were well-intentioned enough to try. No, to make a movie like this you need to go to Regina, Saskatchewan, and you need to go there in the winter. And you need non-traditional relationships with actors who are brave enough to follow you to Saskatchewan. In the winter... The script for this movie was written on an old busted laptop covered with* Star Trek *stickers as my own world was turning upside down, and really that's the only way it could have been written. I pulled most of the set out of a dumpster with the help of five confused house movers and a French documentarian who owed me a favor and put a tarp over it for a year. I met up with academics, astronauts, NASA experts in the science of orbital debris. People who did science. That's where all the science came from. I also watched every movie with a robot in it. And every movie that took place in space. And every episode of television with aliens. But I would have done that anyway. The point is that I wanted to get it right, but at the end of the journey from idea to production, getting it right wasn't about science, or the sexy aliens, or even the homicidal robots, but always the story of the little guy*". Talk about overhype a product! ("That's where all the science came from" indeed! What science?!) Incidentally, since I last visited its page at the IMDb, **SM**'s user rating there has since inexplicably drastically skyrocketed to a whopping "7.8" on the Sphincter Scale (when I originally looked back last year sometime, it was at the even then still-much-too-generous "6.0"). I am now thoroughly convinced there is no hope for civilization! I mean, it's good for a few laughs and all, but, Canadian or not, it ain't *that* good.

SUBURBAN GOTHIC (p.71) – This film's theatrical world premiere was at Montreal's Fantasia International Film Festival in July 2014, and it was also screened at the Toronto After Dark Film Festival (in Oct '14), receiving its general US theatrical release on January 30, 2015. It is currently available for rental or purchase as an Amazon Instant Video in either HD or SD quality modes. For some reason, as of this writing—possibly an error?—both options are priced exactly the same (@ $6.99 to rent and $9.99 to buy). **SG** is also viewable VOD via iTunes and FilmBuff (*www.filmbuff.com*).

TERRORVISION (p.49) – Issued on Blu-ray by Shout! Factory in 2013 as part of their horrorcentric Scream Factory line, double-billed with Robert Scott's zombie flick **THE VIDEO DEAD** (1987, USA). Both films are also available on Blu separately from the same company. Back during the '80s/'90s home vid boom, **TV** was put out on VHS/Beta cassette by Lightning/Vestron Video.

TO THE DEVIL A DAUGHTER (p.83) – The film is currently rentable/purchasable as an Amazon insta-vid, but only in SD quality mode (at $2.99 to rent or $6.99 to buy). It was issued on domestic DVD (now OOP) by Anchor Bay in 2002, and on PAL Region 2 (UK) DVD by StudioCanal in 2004. To date, so far as we can tell, it hasn't been released anywhere on Blu-ray.

TWINS OF EVIL (p.80) – Released on domestic Blu-ray in 2013 by Synapse Films. The numerous extras with that edition include a feature-length documentary entitled **THE FLESH AND THE FURY: X-POSING THE TWINS OF EVIL**.

VAMPIRE CIRCUS (p.81) – Released on domestic Blu-ray in 2010 by Synapse Films. Their edition comes with many extras, including: *The Bloodiest Show On Earth*: "Making Vampire Circus" – An all-new documentary featuring interviews with writer/director Joe Dante, Hammer documentarian Ted Newsom, *Video Watchdog* editor/author Tim Lucas, author/film historian

Philip Nutman, and actor David Prowse; *Gallery of Grotesqueries*: "A Brief History of Circus Horrors" – A retrospective on circus/carnival-themed horror productions; *Visiting the House of Hammer*: "Britain's Legendary Horror Magazine" – A retrospective on the popular British horror/comic publication, featuring author Philip Nutman; and *Vampire Circus*: an interactive comic book, featuring artwork by Brian Bolland.

MUTANO LIVES!
... SORt OF.

WHO (OR *WHAT*) IS (OR *WAS*) THE MYSTERIOUS "MUTANO"?!

Whoever/whatever the hell **MUTANO THE HORRIBLE** was—and possibly (hopefully!) still is?—that tantalizing "teaser" title mentioned repeatedly in ancient issues of *Famous Monsters* has had Monster Kids the world over scratching their oversized foreheads ever since (see also Steve Bissette's mention of **MTH** on p.27). Over the intervening decades, it has taken on an almost mythic status among those who care about such stuff (*ehhh*, I guess that includes us). But, we can only wonder, did it ever actually exist as a bona fide film, or was it perhaps just some wishful-thinking, phony-baloney title concocted by the infamously punny Forry Ackerman for laughs? *FM* was notorious for exaggerating sometimes—often in the interests of making a cheap pun—and there were times when the mag put simple sensationalism before actual factual veracity, I think. So possibly this mystery title was merely a made-up one

WHat IS THE TRUTH ? TURn tHE PaGE, WE DaRE YOU!

This intriguing shot is apparently from **EXPERIMENTS OF YALON**

attached to a still for wont of anything better to caption it with? Then again…

After *Monster!*'s own Tim P. posted the poser "So, what's the poop on **MUTANO THE HORRIBLE**?" on Facebook a few days ago, he received some interesting nuggets from a couple respondents, including several from John Donaldson; Gordon Jackson kindly provided pertinent links to some pic-

The late Walter Lee's essential *Reference Guide to Fantastic Films: Science Fiction, Fantasy, & Horror, volume 1 A–F*

tures (scanned out of *FM*) from Tumblr. Mr. Donaldson cited the late Walt Lee's (1931-2014) epic, 3-volume *Reference Guide To Fantastic Films: Science Fiction, Fantasy, & Horror* (LA: Chelsea-Lee Books, 1973) as having listed **MUTANO** (dating from 1961?) in its section of problematic titles; as possibly being the work of a West German producer of amateur films named Klaus Unbehaun, who is known as a prolific published author of reference books, often about trick photography and special effects or related subjects. His published works include *Filmtricks-ABC: Ein Werkbuch für begeisterte Film-amateure* (Munich: Gemsberg Verlag, 1967), *Fototricks als Hobby* (Knapp Verlag, 1978), and *Filmtitel, -schnitt und -montage: klipp und klar!* (Munich: Gemsberg Verlag, 1973). At least one of his books was published in a 1962 Italian edition by Milan's Il Castello imprint (as part of its "*Biblioteca del cineamatore* / Amateur Film Library" series) under the title *Trucchi ed effetti per I vostri film* / "Tricks and Effects For Your Movies". One of the author's more recent works—at least we're assuming they are the same person, as Unbehaun doesn't appear to be an overly common German surname—is *Profitipps für Modellbahndiorahmen* (Transpress Verlag, 2008), which roughly translates to "Pro Tips About Model Train Dioramas". As of this writing, used copies of all these above-cited (mostly presumably now OOP?) books were being offered for sale at various online sites, including eBay.

Being as how Unbehaun was evidently both born and based in Germany, possibly **MUTANO THE HORRIBLE** might just have been a loose Anglicization of a German title? (Which may have been *"Mutano die schrecklichen"*, or some similar variation thereof?) So many questions!

According to Steve Bissette, film scholar Bill Warren informed him, "It was a German amateur movie that I think was never completed—if I remember correctly what Forry told me". The above-cited Mr. Donaldson also mentioned that Lee's *Reference Guide* even lists a supposed sequel to **MUTANO**[1] under the English title **EXPERIMENTS OF YALON** (1966), with the name Charles MacDonald attached to it as part of the cast. On FB, Donaldson remarked to Tim, "Back when I was a teenager, I remember *Famous Monsters* publishing a couple of stills from one or the other, and the title has always stuck with me". Although we are here formatting their titles as though they are (were?) full-length feature films, more than likely they might only have been short subjects shot on either 8mm or 16mm film? Again, so *many* questions!! But judging by the number of "how-to" guides Unbehaun wrote on the topic of amateur filmmaking, it seems highly likely that the non-professional "Outsider" fringes may have been their source of origin... assuming that either/or of them actually ever got completed, that is. But we can only hope copies might pop up on YouTube sometime soon! Better late than never, as they say. ~**SF**

---

1 At Monster Kid Memories > The Lopsided Eyes Have It! (The Official Lopsided Eye Monster Thread of the Classic Horror Film Board [*monsterkidclassichorrorforum.yuku.com*]), someone calling themselves Carbon gave the release year as 1968 and mentioned seeing a brief description of the film which said: "thriller of a town terrorized by a teen-age monster-maker, his ghoul and a nocturnal vampire".

Klaus Unbehaun
Fototricks als Hobby
Ein Knapp Fotobuch

klaus unbehaun

trucchi ed effetti per i vostri film

realizzazione tecnica e sfruttamento

biblioteca del cineamatore 2

Filmtricks-Abc

Ein Werkbuch für begeisterte Filmer von Klaus Unbehaun

Filmtricks-ABC

Ein Werkbuch für begeisterte Filmer von Klaus Unbehaun

Filmtitel, -schnitt und -montage

klipp und klar!

von Klaus Unbehaun

Ein Lehrbuch für Filmer, die mehr aus ihrem Hobby machen wollen ...

Printed in Great Britain
by Amazon

25633767R00061